Why are the mayors all quitting?

Why are the cities all broke?

Why are the people all angry?

Why are we dying of smoke?

Why are the streets unprotected?

Why are the schools in distress?

Why is the trash uncollected?

How did we make such a mess?

—Anonymous
from "Beyond the Machine"
by Edward N. Costikyan

Governing the City examines the major personalities, problems, and possible cures for the urban dilemma from its beginnings in the early 1900s to the present.

Governing the City
is an original POCKET BOOK edition.

PROBLEMS OF AMERICAN SOCIETY

Focusing on the urban scene, youth, the individual and his search for a better life, the books in this series probe the most crucial dilemmas of our time.

* Forthcoming

GERALD
LEINWAND

Governing
the
City

PUBLISHED BY POCKET BOOKS NEW YORK

GOVERNING THE CITY

POCKET BOOK edition published October, 1971

This original POCKET BOOK edition is printed from
brand-new plates made from newly set, clear, easy-to-read type.
POCKET BOOK editions are published by POCKET BOOKS, a division of
Simon & Schuster, Inc., 630 Fifth Avenue, New York, N.Y. 10020.
Trademarks registered in the United States and other countries.

L

ACKNOWLEDGMENT

For their participation the author wishes to thank the authors and publishers who permitted their articles to be reproduced here. I am in debt also to the many with whom selected portions of the manuscript were discussed. The cooperation of the editorial staff of POCKET BOOKS was indispensable to the successful completion of the volume. I am deeply grateful.

Preface

In this series on urban problems an attempt has been made to identify significant paradoxes and dilemmas of urban life. Thus, one volume considered the paradox of poverty in the midst of affluence. Another reviewed the dilemmas of public transit vs. the private automobile. A third focused on the dilemma of the Negro in finding a secure place in urban society. Problems of slums, of crime, of delinquency, of air and water pollution have all been examined. In many ways, however, the key to the solution of these problems rests in the kind of local government this nation has, and on the relationships of local government to state and national government. Politics has been described as the art of the possible. And it is from the politics of local, state, and national government that possible solutions to the dilemmas and paradoxes of urban life may emerge.

Governing the City is an introductory study. It seeks to introduce the reader to the dilemma of trying to provide a higher level of public services against a background of rising costs for such services and a declining tax base. It attempts to explain, in simple fashion, the paradox that arises from the rural frame of reference of state legislatures and the urban environment in which the overwhelming majority of the people live. These problems are highly complex. This volume has endeavored to present the

problems simply, without being simplistic. It is hoped
that those who read this book will acquire not only
better insight into the problems of local government,
but may also find in local government, either as
elected officials or as civil servants, a fruitful avenue
for the expression of their interests and talents.

As do other volumes in the "Problems of American Society" series, this book begins with a brief
overview of the problems of urban government.
Following are fifteen selected, annotated readings
that examine different points of view and acquaint
the reader with a variety of sources. Neither the
overview nor the readings attempt to provide answers. Instead, they raise questions, create doubts,
and encourage further study and inquiry into the
problems. Some readings are simple. Others are
more sophisticated. This is but an introductory
study and can only be a beginning of an
examination of a complex problem.

G. L.

Contents

Contents

Part One

The Problem and the Challenge

FOR people of the city to live well, many vital services are required. Garbage must be collected and pure water must be provided. The streets must be made safe, and the children must be sent to school. Transportation must be rapid, cheap, and efficient. Since man does not live by bread alone, there must be ample room for play and recreation, and adequate facilities for entertainment. Opportunities must be made for cultural enrichment in the form of free museums and libraries.

Most of these services are provided by city governments. For many of them, the city is helped by the national and state governments. While national and state governments touch us very closely, it is the local government, in the form of city, county, town, and village governments, that has traditionally been closest to the people. Before there was the nation, there were local governments. The states of today were the colonies of yesterday. The national government came into being only because the colonies were willing to give up to it some of their powers so that the greater good of all might be served.

One of the dilemmas of urban life today is that the services cities are being asked to perform are not being performed well enough. There is fear that these services are becoming too costly and that the city is unable to pay for them. As cities grow, their people spill out into suburban and into exurban areas. Metropolitan regions embrace many forms of local government and even cross state lines. The problems of providing essential services become increasingly complex. Who should provide the services the people need? How shall the services be paid for? And who shall pay? And how much should each pay? Since services performed by the government must be paid for by taxes, who should be taxed, what should be taxed, and how much should the tax be? Writing in the 1880s, a famous British observer of the American political scene, James Bryce, declared that city government was the great American failure. In those days it was corruption in city government that worried him most. Today, there is worry that cities have become so large, so complex, and so costly that they are just ungovernable. If this should be true, then the plight of the city is dangerous indeed. But let us see.

How Do Local Governments Get Their Power?

In Article I, Section 8 of the Constitution of the United States may be found a list of the powers of Congress. Amendment X, the last amendment in the Bill of Rights, specifically provides that "the powers not delegated to the United States by the Constitution, nor prohibited by it to the States, are reserved to the States respectively, or to the people." What this meant, at the time the Constitution

Ridiculous, Isn't It?

This cartoon by Frank Williams first appeared in the *Detroit Free Press* on February 16, 1945. It appeared again on January 24, 1969. It seems things haven't changed much. (Frank L. Williams, Detroit Free Press)

was written, was that the national government would be one of limited powers. Its powers would include only those specifically listed in Article I, Section 8 of the Constitution; such powers as control over the commerce between states and with foreign countries, the power to raise an army, to borrow and coin money, to declare war and make peace. With the exception of a few things that the states were expressly forbidden to do, all the rest of the possible powers of government were left to the states, and through the state to the local communities themselves.

It may be said, however, that as the nation became older and as our society became more complex, the ideas of the writers of the Constitution did not work out the way they had planned. Instead of local government having the most power, the national government became the most powerful. The national government regulates minimum wages and maximum hours of labor. It taxes incomes and provides for social security. It regulates commerce and traffic between the states. It regulates the buying and selling of stocks and bonds. It regulates public utilities, such as electricity. It controls the waterways and navigation on them and the high seas. The result has been the growth of one very strong national government and many weak state and local governments.

While the Constitution provides that contracts and agreements made in one state be binding in another, states have often gone their own way. A driver licensed in one state must obtain a new driver's license by passing a new test if he moves to another state. Divorce laws vary substantially, divorce being easily obtainable for a resident of Nevada, but difficult to obtain for a resident of New York. What may be a crime in one state is not one in another. Laws regarding compulsory schooling and the quality of that schooling likewise vary significantly.

Thus, one of the major characteristics of government in the United States is its variety and number. It is in the government of the village, town, county, and city that the greatest variety appears. One of the dilemmas of urban life today is whether or not such variety is desirable or efficient. Who's in charge when powers of local governments overlap? Does urban living today require new forms of local government? Who should be primarily responsible for showing the way, for taking the lead in pointing out new directions for local government?

Is the Variety of Local Government Too Great?

A metropolitan area may be defined as a central city with its suburbs. Metropolitan New York consists of more than New York City. It is made up of nine counties in New Jersey (Hudson, Essex, Union, Passaic, Bergen, Monmouth, Middlesex, Somerset, and Morris), as well as twelve in New York (the five boroughs or counties making up New York City proper, and Nassau, Suffolk, Westchester, Rockland, Orange, Putnam, and Dutchess counties), and one county, Fairfield, in Connecticut. In this area may be found 1,467 distinct and separate kinds of political units, ". . . each having its own power to raise and spend the public treasure and each operating in a jurisdiction determined more by chance than design."[1]

Within this area will be found such local governments as that of cities, counties, boroughs, towns, and villages. Also in this area may be found such special and limited "governments" as school districts, water districts, and fire districts. In addition, one will also find nearly self-governing units such as the Port of New York Authority, the Triborough Bridge and Tunnel Authority, and the Metropolitan Transit Authority. These governments exist side by side and perform overlapping duties. Highways, tax collection, public works, welfare and planning, and the administration of justice are usually the responsibility of county governments. However, when a city is located within a county, then the right to make laws in these areas usually belongs to the city. Towns often issue licenses, pass zoning laws, and provide for parks, playgrounds, and recreation. Villages often share many of these activities with towns and sometimes have duties of their own, including the local control and regulation of traffic. It is all but impossible to say with precision just what each local unit of government does. A family living in the suburbs may be sending a child to one school district and pay taxes to quite a different town or village.

Such variety may be good. It suggests democracy. In small local units of government, residents can take part in regulating their own affairs. Overlapping of powers provides a system of checks and balances and prevents any one part of government from becoming too powerful. It may make for a government that is more responsive to the needs and wishes of the people.

On the other hand, such variety may be bad. Because the units of local government are so small, no one unit is large enough, strong enough, nor rich enough to solve the problems the metropolitan area faces. Because the units are so small, no one unit of government may be willing to undertake needed changes. Because units of government are so small, jobs that need doing may remain undone. There may be a tendency to delay and to postpone in hopes that either the problem will go away, or that the state or federal government will step in to do the job and pay the bill, or that the people themselves will outgrow the need they had. How to rid themselves of too many local governments is one of the problems facing metropolitan areas today.

What Are the Forms of City Government?

A city may be regarded as a creature of the state, that is, it is the state that creates the city and gives the city its powers. While states may do anything not specifically forbidden by the United States Constitution, city governments may do only what is allowed them by the state constitutions.

Among the main forms that city governments may take, the following are the most important: (1) the mayor-council; (2) the commission; and (3) the council-manager.

The mayor-council type of government is most popular in the United States. Under this form the chief executive is the mayor. He is helped by a lawmaking body usually consisting of a single house. In New York City the lawmaking body is the city council. The board of estimate also plays a role in some legislative procedures. The members of the council are usually elected by the people for various periods of time. In New York City, councilmen serve for four years. The board of estimate is made up of the mayor, the comptroller, the president of the council, and the presidents of the five boroughs. In this form of city government, the mayor is an official elected by the people for a fixed number of years.

The mayor-council form of city government may be of two general types. The mayor may have great powers. He may be responsible for the administration of the city and have the power to govern the city with but minimum need to get approval from the council. In other cases, the mayor may be a figurehead and may participate on ceremonial occasions, but the real power is in the hands of the city council. Most of the mayor-council forms of city government work with a strong mayor. Los Angeles, however, may be regarded as an example of a city with a weak mayor in a mayor-council form of government.

It was in Galveston, Texas, in 1901, that the commission form of city government was born. While Birmingham, Alabama; Memphis, Tennessee; and Omaha, Nebraska, are among the cities that still have the commission form of government, this type of government is no longer held to be as effective as it was once thought to be. The commission form of government came into existence as a partial answer to the problems of corruption in city government, usually in the mayor-council arrangement. It was felt that if a city were governed by a commission of three to five men, elected by the people, there would be fewer opportunities for corruption to take place. In this form of government, the commissioners are both the law-enforcing as well as the lawmaking body of the city.

Lawmaking and law enforcement located in one body may be desirable. It makes prompt action possible. Because the commissioners are relatively few in number, they can meet readily and decide on what to do. On the other hand, not every commissioner is an able administrator. It takes one kind of ability to know what laws a city requires and another to

Creativity is essential in city government. Play areas have to be created even when there is no space available. (Peter Vadnai)

know how to carry out those laws. Moreover, in a body which is responsible for both law enforcement and lawmaking, there is no system of checks and balances. Bad laws, when inexpertly enforced, can lead to chaos and confusion.

In 1908, the city of Staunton, Virginia, devised the city-manager plan of city government. This form of government may be said to grow out of the need of the city for experts to decide what needs to be done. A city is a corporation and as such is concerned with the technical problems of providing water and housing and sanitation. There is the problem of planning for city growth, and of providing for transportation and traffic. Problems of pollution,

Free entertainment, especially in ghetto areas, provides relief from depressive poverty and slum existence. (Marion Faller, Monkmeyer)

of slums, of welfare, require a person who knows something about the technical aspects of these problems. Not every elected commissioner, and certainly not every elected mayor, can be expected to know the complicated aspects of these problems.

Under the city-manager plan, the city council, elected by the people, chooses a city manager. They choose him on the basis of his ability to solve the problems the city faces. The city council, sometimes including a weak mayor, makes policy. The skilled city manager is responsible for carrying out that policy and for taking those steps that may be needed to make the government of the city efficient and effective. The council-manager form of govern-

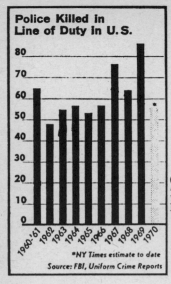

Police Killed in Line of Duty in U.S.

80
70
60
50
40
30
20
10
0

1960-'61 1962 1963 1964 1965 1966 1967 1968 1969 1970

*NY Times estimate to date
Source: FBI, Uniform Crime Reports

(Copyright © 1970 by *The New York Times.* Reprinted by permission.)

Who is the policeman today? Does he still wear this uniform, or has it been replaced by a helmet, short jacket, and riot club? (Ted Kimmel, Monkmeyer)

Will an increased show of police force calm a troubled area? Is there any other way to approach this problem? (Wide World)

ment is gaining in popularity. Cincinnati, Ohio, and Dallas, Texas, are among the larger cities using it.

What Services Do Local Governments Provide?

The American city-dweller depends upon his municipality for many services. So many, in fact, that what the city does perform is so commonplace and familiar that he and his fellow urbanites do not pause to appreciate the real extent to which city services have become a part of their daily lives.

Police Protection

Police protection is probably the first service that is expected of local government. In towns, such protection is provided by the constable. In the village, it may be provided by a person called the marshal. Often, in such small communities, there is but one constable or one marshal in the entire town or village. He is probably not well trained for his job, but he does have the responsibility of trying to protect the town or village. He may be asked to arrest a person believed to be a criminal, or he may direct traffic during the Fourth of July parade. He may give a parking or speeding ticket to the traveling salesman who rushes through the village on his way to the big city beyond. The constable or marshal may serve notices to appear in local court. The movie Westerns have made the office of sheriff appear important. Actually, a sheriff is the police officer of a county. Usually he is concerned with the enforcement of law and order in rural areas. Where a large city is located in a county, there the sheriff often has little to do.

The official of city government seen most often is undoubtedly the policeman. Dressed in a special uniform, the police officer may direct traffic. He may give out parking or speeding tickets. He patrols his beat on foot or cruises in a patrol car. Policemen have three main jobs: to enforce laws; to prevent crimes; and, where the police officer has been unsuccessful in preventing crime, to find and arrest criminals. Police services have become highly specialized. There are some policemen who deal only with narcotics addicts, and others, detectives, whose job it is to ascertain the whereabouts of a criminal. There are policemen who work in laboratories and others who operate radios or pilot helicopters. Some specialize in finding missing persons, and some work with boys in a Police Athletic League. And there are policewomen who have specialized jobs of many kinds, often dealing with women who have committed a crime.

The increased rate of crime in cities has focused attention on the police. Theirs is a difficult and dangerous job. It requires gentleness to lead children across the street, yet physical courage to subdue violent criminals. In between, there are many degrees of force that the policeman must apply. The police have been accused of applying too much force when dealing with a race riot or a demonstration of adults or students who oppose the policies of the government. While the people have a right to peacefully demonstrate and protest, the police have an obligation to protect the rest of the community who may not wish to participate. Sometimes, in judging how much force to exert, some individual policemen may use poor judgment and exercise too much force. Police departments of any large city must be trained

A fire in one building can destroy a whole city block.
(Wide World)

to act with restraint and care, even under the most provocative conditions.

Fire Protection

When man discovered fire, he took one great step up the ladder of civilization. But fire has also been one of man's worst enemies. Particularly has it been the enemy of the city. In ancient times, Rome was destroyed by fire. And during the seventeenth century a great fire destroyed much of London. In 1871, a fire destroyed much of Chicago. Because in a city people live close to one another, the danger from fire has always been great. The fireman's job in small communities remains a voluntary one. That is, a group of men volunteer to man the fire-fighting equipment of a village. When they hear a signal, they rush down to the station where the equipment is kept and rush to the fire without delay.

In a large city, dependence upon volunteers is unsatisfactory. Instead, a city must rely on well-trained professionals whose job is the prevention of fire, the inspection of buildings for the elimination of fire dangers, and the putting out of fires when they occur. Firemen have the responsibility of saving the lives of those endangered by fire, and of trying to provide emergency first-aid to those hurt by fires.

Fire-fighting today is a highly specialized affair. The equipment is expensive and highly technical. In putting out a fire, one must know when to use water and when to use chemicals. The fire department, like the police department, is a quasi-military force, that is, the men are organized into battalions and are under the orders of a chief. These orders must

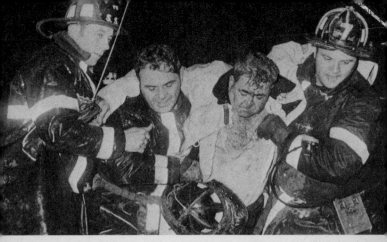

Fire fighting in the city is a full-time profession and in fact a science of its own. (UPI)

be obeyed without delay, very much as soldiers must obey the orders of their commanding officer.

Health Protection

The health of any city is protected in several ways. We look to the city to provide us with pure water, to dispose of garbage efficiently so that disease is not spread, to provide sewage facilities so that human and animal wastes can be drained out of the city. Most cities have laws regarding the sale of food and the protection of the food that is sold. There are departments of health and hospitals that operate public hospitals and try to provide vaccines and effective medical aid for all the people, especially the poor, who can afford no other medical care. The health department will also try to fight rats, roaches, flies, and mosquitoes, when these are dangerous to the health of the city. They publish booklets which are widely distributed and teach families

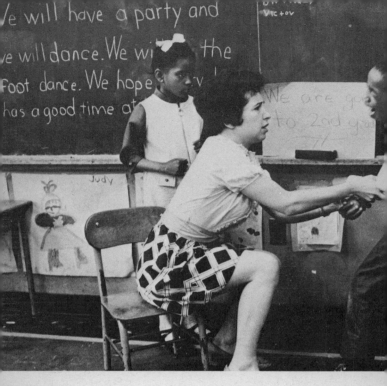

how to care for themselves and prevent sickness and disease from striking.

In large cities the removal of rubbish, the furnishing of pure water, the protection of health, and the operation of public hospitals are all entrusted to large agencies which employ hundreds of men and women. Sometimes, these agencies are headed by a commissioner or other officer appointed by the mayor and responsible to him. Where there is a city manager, it is to the city manager that these officials must generally report.

Effective teaching in ghetto schools requires patience and dedication. A teacher must gain the trust and respect of her pupils. The city must pay to recruit talented educators. (Joe Molnar)

Education

Today, providing free, tax-supported education is regarded as a proper responsibility of government everywhere in the United States. Public education is, in many ways, the most important business of local government. Increasingly, it has become an important part of the business of the federal government as well. State constitutions make the state responsible for providing for its schools. However, the day-to-day regulation of school affairs is left

largely to local units. These units may be as large
as the city itself, as in the case of New York City,
or as small as a village or town. Often, there are
school districts that attempt to combine the elemen-
tary or secondary schools of a wide area into a
single system in order to organize the educational
resources of the area for more efficient education of
the young.

Probably few areas of city effort have come under
more attack than its schools. Schools have been
accused of not doing an effective job of teaching
the newcomers to the city. How to make the schools
responsive to the needs of the cities' racial minorities is a major problem. Integrating the schools to
reduce the concentration of any one race in a school
is certainly another major problem. Such integration
conflicts head-on with the idea of neighborhood
schools which is based on the belief that children
should attend the school nearest their homes. When
the neighborhood school exists, it takes on the pattern of the population near it. While the law may
make segregation in schools illegal, *de facto* segregation—segregation in fact—continues to exist in
the schools of most large cities.

Because of new means available for teaching, and
because of more expensive buildings and higher
salaries for teachers, the costs of education have
increased greatly. Moreover, while at one time children left school at fourteen or earlier, today they
are expected to stay in school much longer. This too
adds to the cost. It also means that the school is now
dealing with many children who simply "dropped
out" before and, as drop-outs, were no longer considered the school's responsibility. Today, the school
tries to prevent drop-outs and tries to work with the
parents to keep them in school. In a highly indus-

trialized nation such as ours, there is little future for those who do not get as much education as they possibly can. Jobs and good wages wait for those with a good education. Unemployment and poverty face those who lack it.

These are but some of the services cities provide. Cities provide parks for recreation and libraries for the advancement of scholarship. They plan for the future and provide for rapid transit into and out of the city. All of the services cities provide have become costly to operate and complex to organize. We have simplified them here so that you will be in a better position to appreciate the role cities play in providing the services needed in order to live. But the problem is that cities are accused of not providing these services as effectively as they might be provided. What is wrong? Why are some services poorer today than they once were? Why does the city appear to be falling behind in providing for the needs of the community?

Why Do People Look to the City for Service?[2]

Nearly everything a city does for its people can be done by private organizations of one kind or another. Thus, city-owned transit facilities compete with those owned by private companies. The city runs some hospitals, but many are privately run. While the city provides schools, many children go to private and parochial schools. The city runs museums and libraries, but there are also some that are privately owned and operated. The famous New York Public Library is substantially supported by private funds. Many corporations provide their own special police, and every business firm pays for carting away its

rubbish. If private organizations can provide these services, why should the city do so?

One reason people look to the city to provide such services as fire and police protection is that adequate protection would be out of reach for most citizens and most firms if only private funds were used. By spreading the cost among many people the expense for each individual becomes very small. Moreover, the city has certain powers that private groups do not have. The city can tax. It can borrow money, usually at favorable interest rates. The city tends to do those things that would not be profitable for private organizations. As a general rule it may be said that ". . . the government gets pushed into ac-

Most of the entertainment that comes to the city is privately sponsored. (Dennis McGuire)

tivities that . . . cannot pay for themselves, and it is often pushed out again as soon as someone scents the possibility of personal gain."[3]

A second reason why people expect the city to provide services is that the city has the authority to force people to do what needs to be done. If public housing must be built in a certain area, the city has the right to take the property (with payment to the owners) and build the necessary apartments. If businesses must maintain sprinkler systems as a means of preventing fires, it is because the city has the power to force them to do so. If traffic can be improved by restricting parking, the city can make people obey the law.

A wise city will be certain to sponsor some free public entertainment that offers a peaceful release from urban tensions. (UPI)

In addition to the two reasons mentioned above, it must be remembered that the city can also be forced or coaxed into performing services for its people that it might prefer not to perform. Those who run the city are, after all, politicians. And politicians, if they wish to win and keep their jobs and their power, must listen to the demands of the people. Political leaders may thus be subjected to pressure. Heads of private businesses cannot be subjected to pressure in the same way or to the same degree. Effective local officials are those who know what services the people need and want, and how to work to provide those services.

Who Provides the Services for the City?

No city can effectively run without the labor of thousands of workers. These include, of course, the elected officials and those appointed to top-level jobs. Just as important, however, are the large numbers of clerical assistants and technical experts upon whom any city of any size depends for the day-to-day efficiency of its activities. Those who work for government—city, state, or federal—are called civil servants. Because they are paid from public funds and because they provide the services the people need, there is great interest in how they get and keep their jobs, as well as what they do.

The higher jobs in government are obtained either by election or by appointment. Usually, the elected official—in the case of most city governments, the mayor—appoints the officials of the major departments. These, in turn, may appoint other executives to help them run the particular department for which they are responsible. However, most of the lower levels today are filled on the basis of a competitive examination and an impartial review of an applicant's qualifications in terms of the requirements for a particular job. This is called the merit system. A list is usually drawn up, listing the successful applicants on the basis of the test results. The higher the grade, the higher up on the list one is likely to be. The higher up on the list, the sooner the applicant is likely to be called for a job.

The merit system was essentially launched in 1883, when Congress passed the Pendleton Act. Its main purpose was to provide a fair way of choosing employees of the federal government. Similar laws have set up merit systems covering many jobs in most cities. A merit system is designed not only to choose able men and women for particular jobs, but to avoid the earlier practice of the spoils system, based on the theory that "to the victor belong the spoils." What is meant is that the spoils of office, in this case jobs, may be handed out on the basis of party favor or loyalty, or family ties or friendship, with little or no regard for ability. It meant that, whenever a new party was elected, all those who were appointed were dismissed, and friends of the winner were appointed instead.

In no city government have we entirely eliminated the spoils system, nor can we. And in no city government does the merit system work as well as it should. When a new party comes into power, there must be some jobs for the party to distribute. It is one way of assuring political party loyalty, and, without political parties, democracy as we know it cannot work. Moreover, it is only reasonable to permit those who have won an election to appoint those who can be relied upon to carry out new and hopefully better policies. As a result, most of the higher jobs in the city, state, or federal government are based on appointment, and there is no need for examinations or for the establishment of particular job requirements. Sometimes even relatively minor jobs are not subject to the merit system.

The merit system, on the other hand, does attempt to identify people of ability for a host of technical and clerical jobs. Some of these jobs may require a very high level of ability indeed. Others may require nothing more than the unskilled labor needed to keep the halls and rooms of a city office building clean and the windows washed. The merit system has much to commend it, and it should be extended to more jobs. But it also needs improvement. For one thing, paper and pencil tests do not always measure such things as industry, initiative, creativity, sincerity, and effort. For another, the knowledge and skills required for some jobs are not easily tested. Often, where they can be tested, the tests can be studied or crammed for, with the result that the candidate who has crammed the most may pass and get the job.

One of the things that usually goes hand-in-hand with a civil service appointment is tenure. That is, after a person has served a trial period, usually up to three years, he gains job security. He cannot be fired, except for the severest reasons, and then not without a formal hearing. As a result, too often those who feel secure in their jobs, because they cannot be fired, do not perform as well as they should. Often the civil service creates a slow-moving bureaucracy which is not responsive to the people, since the people will not be called upon to reelect them to office. In addition, partially because of tenure, salaries in civil service jobs have usually been somewhat lower than salaries paid for similar jobs in private industry. Because salaries are lower, the best people prefer jobs in private industry rather than in municipal government.

Should Civil Servants Be Allowed to Strike?

One of the real problems in municipal government

The strength of civil service strikes lies in the ability to interfere in the functions of big business. Big business is the heart of the city and the city cannot sustain its life without it. (Wide World)

today is that of the right of civil servants to join a union and to strike for higher wages, better working conditions, and shorter hours. In most places, laws have been passed making it illegal for civil servants to strike. These laws have been difficult to enforce as more civil servants have joined labor unions and have gone on strike. Teachers, transit workers, sanitation workers, welfare workers, postal workers, and policemen all have struck for improvement in their working conditions and salaries in recent years.

As public servants, it is reasonable to expect that they should not strike against the public. There is no "boss" in the usual sense of the term. Salaries can be improved only by raising taxes, not by raising prices. No one works for profit. On the other hand, it is reasonable to expect that civil servants will join unions and will want to strike to improve themselves, since their opposite numbers in private industry do so, and do improve their lot faster than those working for government. Why an elevator operator in a municipal building—who is a civil servant—should not be permitted to strike, while one in a private building may do so, is not an easy question to answer. The same is true for bus drivers and maintenance men.

Among the more sensitive questions is whether or not police and fire department employees should be allowed to join unions and to strike. Since they are members of a quasi-military organization, it is reasonable to expect them not to, as such a strike would be against the public safety. However, teachers have gone on strike and there are likely to be more strikes by teachers in the future. Since they are not members of a military establishment, is a strike by teachers justified? Does such a strike hurt the children? Can they be prevented from striking by law? So far the laws preventing such strikes have not been effective. Yet it may be said that the public interest is hurt by any work stoppage, whether it be by the drivers who deliver milk to babies, or teachers who instruct their big brothers and sisters. On the other hand, in a democracy, every worker at any level has the right to try to improve the conditions under which he works. Collective bargaining, in which a strike is one of the weapons used as a last resort, has been guaranteed by law. It is one of the strengths of democracy and one of the signs of a democratic nation.

Why Has It Become Increasingly Difficult for Cities to Provide the Services People Need?

Most people today live in metropolitan areas. While not everyone lives in the central city, nevertheless the overwhelming majority of the people live in, or near, big cities. As we have seen, every metropolitan area is made up of a large number of governments. These may be city governments, village governments, town governments, county or borough governments. We have noted that the powers of these governments are not clear. They overlap. Many have

Garbage strikes not only leave a mess in the city streets, but also create a health hazard. (Wide World)

no real reason for existing, other than the fact that they have been in existence for many years. This fragmentation of political jurisdictions may be regarded as the most serious obstacle in any attempt to provide the people with the services they need. For example, the streets and roads of a city do not begin or end at the city boundary. Instead, they are closely tied to a network of state highways, and involve bridges and tunnels. If traffic congestion in the city is to be eliminated or improved substantially, then it is clear that much depends on what is done on the highways leading into the city and on those leading out of it. Much depends upon the bridges

Highway traffic jams in and around major metropolitan areas are taken for granted. Until mass transportation is humanized this problem will continue to plague our cities. (Wide World)

and tunnels that are provided. The highways leading into and out of the city run through various forms of local governments. Each has some limited authority over the segment of road that runs through the area which it governs.

Many of the highways are built with state and federal funds. For a highway to be built from Manhattan in New York City to the tip of Long Island, the approval of many governments, each with different ideas and needs and interests, must be sought. As a result, it often takes an unduly long period of time before agreement can be reached. In the meantime, the problem remains. When a solution is finally agreed upon and carried out, it is often already out of date. The highway is already inadequate. Congestion persists, as it did before.

The same thing is true for a host of other government services. If air pollution is a problem in a metropolitan area, no one city or community can solve that problem by itself. Instead, it must obtain the cooperation of every other city and community in the metropolitan area. New York's air, for example, cannot be made pure unless the State of New Jersey does something about the chemical plants that line the New Jersey Turnpike around Elizabeth. And the reverse is true: New Jersey's air cannot be pure unless New York City does something about the smokestacks from the plants that generate electricity for the city.

What is said about pure air is also true with regard to pure water. The water in New York City cannot be either pure enough or adequate unless there is opportunity to regulate the water in reservoirs many miles from the city. If those living nearer the supply of water use it to sprinkle their lawns, those living

Pollution must be recognized as the enemy of all mankind. It cannot be fought by each state claiming the other is responsible. We are all responsible. (Sam Falk, Monkmeyer)

in the city may have little water to drink. But who can control the use of water in communities outside of New York City?

In the case of the disposal of rubbish, similar problems apply. Much of the rubbish gathered in the city is dumped outside it. Where should it be dumped? If it is dumped outside, then it is dumped in or near a community that has laws and regulations of its own. Much rubbish is used to fill in land, and then the land is used for homes or apartments. But when there is no more place to dump the rubbish, what should be done with it? The next best answer seems to be to burn it. But where should the incinerators be located? How can the smoke from the incinerators be controlled so that the air of the city is not polluted? If the incinerators are located in the suburbs, then is the air of suburbia being polluted by the rubbish of the central city?

A real headache to metropolitan areas is the airport. Bus and railroad terminals are usually located in the heart of the central city. Taxis, trains, or local buses serve those people deposited at the terminal and take them to their ultimate destination. In the case of airports the reverse is true. The central city is dependent upon airports. But the airport must be located in the suburb. Because of the noise of jets and the pollution brought about by jet fuels, few suburban communities are willing to have airports. Where should an airport be located? How should passengers be moved from the air terminal to the central city? What roads should connect the airport to the city and who should build, pay for, and maintain them?

It is obvious from this brief survey that one of the underlying problems of local government today is how to bring about closer cooperation among the various forms of local government. This raises the question of whether or not all existing forms of local government need to continue to exist. If not, what replaces them? Who decides which will remain and which will not? If they all remain, how can their powers serve to complement and strengthen the provision of services that every metropolitan area needs? These are some of the dilemmas of providing an adequate level of satisfactory service for the people of the metropolitan area.

Why Has It Become Increasingly Difficult for Cities to Pay for the Services People Need?

The problem of providing services needed by the people of the metropolitan area is obviously closely related to the problem of paying for them. Paying for services is closely tied to the problem of taxation. In recent years, it has become increasingly difficult for cities to pay for the services people need. This is because the number of and the demand for better quality in services have increased and costs have been mounting, while the sources of revenue have been falling.

The sources of revenue available to a city are few in number. By far the most important one is the tax on real estate. Those who own homes pay this tax on the basis of the worth (assessed valuation) of their home. The city determines the valuation and then charges the homeowner a percentage of each $100 of its valuation. Those who rent apartments pay the tax as part of their rents. Until recently, the property or real estate tax was almost the only source of revenue for the city. Not only do homeowners pay the tax on the homes they own, but business pays the tax on the property it owns as well.

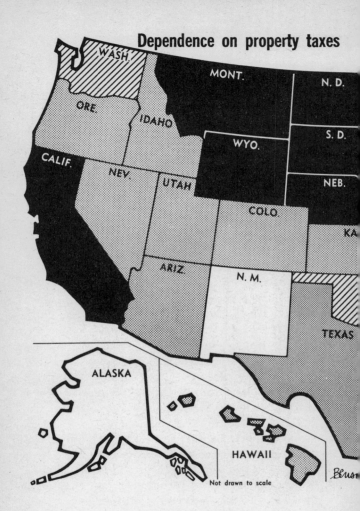

Dependence on property taxes

(1965-1966)

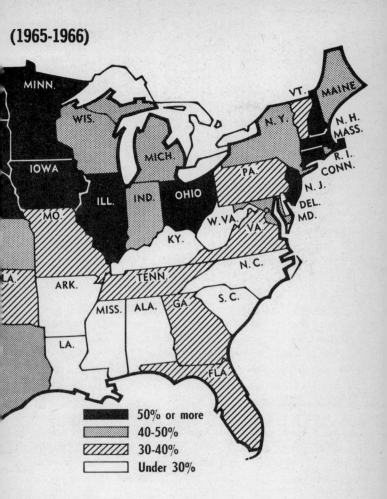

50% or more
40-50%
30-40%
Under 30%

However, for some years the real estate tax has not been providing the city with the revenue it needs. Why not? For one thing, as the middle class bought homes, it bought them in the suburbs. Every time a person from the central city buys a home in the suburbs he takes his taxes with him, and that source of revenue is lost to the city. In the central city, slums, which yield few taxes, have been growing as middle class areas have been declining. As a result, the so-called property tax base, on which cities depend for the revenues they need to provide the services the people of the city require, is being squeezed.

Moreover, what is true for the individual is also true for business. Many businesses today no longer find that it is absolutely necessary for them to remain in the city. They too can move to the suburbs and enjoy the benefits of long, low buildings and park-like surroundings. When they move out, they too take their taxes with them. Although the middle class and much business may move out, the amount of services that the city is called upon to provide continues to increase. Slums, for example, provide little revenue, but need many more services.

Because of the need to raise revenues on sources other than property, cities have looked about for other forms of taxation. They have found these in the city income tax and the sales tax. The income tax is the chief form of revenue for the federal government. Both the city and the state have been looking increasingly to the income tax as a means of adding to their revenue. Residents of New York City now pay a city, state, and federal income tax. Another source of revenue for cities is the sales tax. States too have used the sales tax as a means of raising revenue. The sales tax has not been regarded

The city cannot collect high taxes on slum areas, so there is a shortage of money to put back into them for improvement. (Rogers, Monkmeyer)

If the landlord renovates the building, property value skyrockets, taxes increase, and only the wealthy can move in. This forces the poor people into another overcrowded slum area somewhere else. (Jim Cron, Monkmeyer)

In New Haven, Connecticut, these former flophouses were restored, but still offer decent dwellings for low-income families. (George Favre)

as a good tax because the rich and poor pay the
same amount, depending upon the amount they buy.
Moreover, the rich can often wait until prices are
lower before they buy and then stock up on taxed
commodities. The poor cannot do this. Nevertheless,
the sales tax is here to stay, and there is likely to be
an increase in its use.

To complicate matters, the costs of providing services are growing. Not only are we in a period of
rising prices, but it has been found that the larger
the city the more costly is the *per capita* (per person) cost of the services provided. Mass cities find
the costs of providing such services as sanitation or
snow removal and traffic control unduly high. What-
ever the cost, whether it be providing schooling or
regulating traffic, the expenses of the bigger cities are
higher than the expenses of smaller cities—to provide
the same services. And, since cities are growing, costs
are mounting. Since people of the city are demanding
more services, not fewer, costs for providing a higher
level of service mount again.

While many people have moved from the central
city to the suburbs and have taken their taxes with
them, they are nevertheless "daytime" residents of
the city. That is, they commute from their suburban
homes to the city via public transit or drive their
cars on city streets. They benefit from the police and
fire protection the city offers and from the garbage
collection the city maintains. Not only must the
central city provide for its "nighttime" residents, but
it must also provide for its swollen population during the day. It is for this reason that New York City
has begun to impose an income tax on those who
work in the city but live outside it. This tax was not
imposed without a long fight. And when the tax
increases—as it will—there is sure to be another

fight. But fighting among the various units of metropolitan government will worsen, not improve, the services the people of the metropolitan areas need. How can cooperation instead of conflict be brought about?

America, as a nation, was born and brought up with the rural myth. That is, until relatively recently it was felt that this nation had bred its people mainly on farms, and that the farm and not the city was the source of its strength. While it is true that in the early days this country was more rural than urban, nevertheless, even from its early days as a republic, cities such as Boston, Philadelphia, New York, and Charleston were the moving forces in the nation. But this rural myth never died. Instead, it grew and has been reflected in national and local governments. Today, most state legislatures are dominated by persons who come from rural areas. Today, the rural areas are over-represented in the lawmaking bodies of most states, while the cities are under-represented. While some Supreme Court decisions have attempted to reverse this trend, the attempt has not yet entirely succeeded.

Because of the over-importance of the rural representatives, most cities do not get their fair share of state aid. For example, Jefferson County in Colorado received more money from the state legislature for its nearly 20,000 pupils than did the city of Denver, Colorado, for its nearly 100,000 children. Similar examples may be found in New York, New Jersey, and elsewhere. Mayor Daley of Chicago said, "The cities and metropolitan areas are the important areas of the country today, but they're still on the low part of the totem pole."[4] In 1985, it is expected that the New York metropolitan region will need $42 billion to provide the services the people need.

It is estimated that this is about twice what the region's many governments can raise under existing laws.[5] Because cities find themselves in a tight financial squeeze, they borrow more. Money borrowed must be repaid with interest. Often, the interest itself amounts to a substantial sum. Sometimes, if the money was borrowed for a long enough period of time, it amounts to more than the original amount borrowed. It is a debt that future generations have to pay. It is a fixed item of interest which cannot be reduced when a city tries to balance future budgets.

How May Metropolitan Areas Solve Their Problems?

In this introductory study, we proposed to raise questions rather than to find the answers. The solution to urban problems must be found in many different ways, not just one. But the two basic problems of metropolitan areas may be summed up as too little money and too many governments. These two problems are closely related.

No city in any metropolitan area can be expected to solve its problems by itself. For one thing, it lacks the resources. For another, the solution usually depends upon what other communities have done. As a result, what metropolitan areas need more than anything else is area-wide planning and perhaps even area-wide government. If the problems of metropolitan areas are to be solved, then bold new forms of local government must be created to replace the existing ones. But, as you have seen, city and local governments are the creatures of the states. The states created them, the states can break them. Obviously, it is up to the states to take the lead in encouraging area-wide planning, even if this means

"Chase Manhattan has to draw the line <u>somewhere</u>, Mr. Mayor!"

(Drawing by Alan Dunn. Copyright © 1966 by The New Yorker Magazine, Inc.)

breaking up some of the local governments that now exist.

The problem of breaking up local governments is really not a new one. In fact, it is rather old. Metropolitan (metro) government was the goal that New York City sought when, in 1898, the boroughs of the city of New York were joined together to form the present city. It was the need to work cooperatively on the problems that these communities (known today as counties) faced that prompted the formation of modern New York. Today, other cities are using a variety of methods to organize some form of metro government.

One form of metro government is the Port of New York Authority. It was created in 1921 by the

states of New York and New Jersey to regulate the
port facilities. Eventually, its uses were expanded so
that it built the Lincoln and Holland tunnels, the
George Washington Bridge, and the Port Authority
Bus Terminal. This is an example of a unit of government that has substantial authority in a limited
area. It tries to provide the services that are needed
in the metropolitan area for the development of the
Port of New York.

Dade County in Florida is another example of an
attempt to create a metro government of another
kind. In Dade County may be found Miami Beach
and a number of other local units of government,
including Coral Gables and Hialeah. The purpose
of the Dade County Metro was to provide effective
control of sewage, zoning, water and traffic for
about twenty-six different kinds of local governments which may be found in the county. So far, it
is too early to tell how effectively the Dade County
experiment is working. But there is evidence of deep
jealousies as each community strives to retain its
power and influence. Each is reluctant to shoulder
what it believes to be the burden of neighboring
communities. Seattle, Washington, and Toronto, Canada, are examples of other cities that are trying
various ways to allow the metro government to work
as a single unit in providing metropolitan services to
all the people in the area, regardless of the particular
local unit of government under which they may live.

Some communities are trying to do today what
New York did more than seventy years ago. Namely,
they are trying to consolidate the many forms of
local government. This is an even more difficult job
than the Dade County plan. It requires, in effect,
that the local governments agree to commit suicide.
It means that all local authority and boundaries are

wiped out and that the government, generally of the largest central city, becomes the government of the metro. Pittsburgh, Cleveland, and Detroit are among the cities that have been moving in this direction. And not very successfully, as the local communities stubbornly hold out for what they believe to be their powers. Under consolidation plans, those who live in local communities which have relatively low taxes refuse to consolidate for fear that they will soon be paying high taxes. Those who live in communities that borrowed little feel they will be paying for the debt of those communities that borrowed a great deal.

There has also been some effort to achieve co-operation among the various forms of local government on a voluntary basis. Thus the Metropolitan Regional Council was established for the New York metropolitan area. It consists of the elected heads of sixteen cities and twenty-one counties of New York, New Jersey, and Connecticut. While the "spirit" appears to be there, the will to cooperate effectively seems to be lacking. The Metropolitan Washington Council of Governments is trying to establish voluntary cooperation among the local governments in the Washington, D.C., metropolitan region. In part, because it had the help of Congress, the cooperation among these governments is generally regarded as good.

So far, efforts at metro government as a solution for the problems of our metropolitan areas have been short on results. The fear of higher taxes, loss of power, the domination by the central city, all have contributed to making metro government and area-wide planning still something for the future rather than for the present. "A lot of our metropolitan problems," said Senator Joseph Clark of Pennsyl-

Due to circumstances beyond our control New York City will be closed until further notice.

WE HOPE THIS DOESN'T INCONVENENCE YOU

New York is the greatest city in the world. It has to be, when you think of what people put up with, and even take in their stride to live here.

For instance, in the past couple of years alone, we've had a garbage strike, a tugboat strike, a teachers strike and a mail strike we shared with the rest of the country.

And if that's not enough, somebody's always digging up Third Avenue during the rush hour.

Subways break down. Commuter trains don't run. Not to mention the water mains that crack with fountainlike regularity.

When we created WINS, the New York area's first all news station, we knew it was getting tough to live in New York—but we didn't know how tough.

What we found was that usually about half the news we report in a day is news that was made in New York. Commuter problems. Wall Street's latest rises or dips. The current demonstration at the U.N. The high cost of food, clothing, housing, and just plain living in New York. Plus of course, our usual quota of big strikes and little aggravations.

So we keep on reporting, 24-hours a day. Because in a city like this that's just how it keeps on happening.

At WINS we bring you *all news all the time.* Fast-paced and in depth—the way New Yorkers want it. Not just the fragments—but the whole story.

The news isn't always good. But it's always there. **1010 WINS NEW YORK RADIO**

(WINS Radio, Westinghouse Broadcasting Company)

vania, "are going to have to get worse before people are prepared to take the measures necessary to make them better."[6]

But how much worse can they get? Aren't they bad enough? It has been said of New York City, "It is no exaggeration . . . to say that New York City exists in a state of chronic bankruptcy. . . . Shortcomings affect every one of the three-hundred-odd services the city pretends to perform for its citizens."[7] Must New York City secede from the state and become the fifty-first state, as some propose, before its problems can be solved? How can metro government be made to work? How can splintering of local governments be made to cease?

There is reason to believe that cities may not be able to solve their problems at all. For example, it has been suggested by some that just as we are beginning to discover the city, "the age of the city seems to be at an end."[8] That is, most of the problems a city faces—pollution, crime, race riots, or drug addiction—are not city problems at all. Instead, they have causes totally outside the city. As a result, it is not unreasonable to look for a solution to these problems outside the city. The city as a place with clearly defined territorial boundaries is vanishing. "We cannot hope to invent local treatments for conditions whose origins are not local in character, nor can we expect territorially defined governments to deal effectively with problems whose causes are unrelated to territory or geography."[9] What new forms of government must be designed for a post-city age?

Part Two

Selected Readings

In this editorial, the author explains that the troubled city is by no means new. The city, described as a "conspicuous failure" by some, has nevertheless become man's habitat. Yet, in many ways it remains the "hope of democracy."

1

The American City Is in Trouble

by JUSTIN KAPLAN

"THE government of cities is the one conspicuous failure of the United States," James Bryce wrote in *The American Commonwealth* in 1888. . . .

Many American cities were crippled by machine politics and organized corruption, New York being the most widely publicized but not necessarily the worst example. Violence was familiar, municipal ser-

From "The American City Is in Trouble," by Justin Kaplan, *The New York Times*, December 9, 1967. Copyright © 1967 by The New York Times Company. Reprinted by permission.

Jacob Riis (1849–1914) was one of the earliest fighters for housing reform.

(Photographs by Jacob A. Riis. The Jacob A. Riis Collection, Museum of the City of New York)

"WHO IS INGERSOLL'S CO?" N.Y. TRIBUNE.   MR. INGERSOLL: "ALLOW ME TO INTRODUCE YOU TO MY Co."

TWO GREAT QUESTIONS.   Th. Nast.

WHO STOLE THE PEOPLE'S MONEY? — DO TELL. N.Y. TIMES.   'TWAS HIM.

THE "RAPID TRANSIT" OF "REFORM" AT ALBANY.

Thomas Nast plagued Boss Tweed with his devastating
cartoons. Tweed and his ring sent threatening letters to
Nast and when that failed to stop him they offered him
$500,000. But Nast continued his battle. (Picture Collec-
tion, The New York Public Library)

vices were at best meager and unreliable, and in some cities such paving as there was consisted of garbage and dead animals.

.   .   .

As a social agency, as an instrument of collective power and responsibility for the common good, the American city had scarcely even begun to exist.

The same year Bryce's book was published, Jacob Riis published the first of those searing slum photographs which brought to the eye and the conscience the indisputable facts of how the other half lived.

.   .   .

Still, many of those who believed that the city was a problem peculiar to democracy also believed that the solution to the problem was (as a favorite slogan went) "not less democracy but more." To mobilize the people to "smash corruption," "throw the rascals out," and build "the City Beautiful" became the holy purpose of reformers all over the country. Leading sporadic insurrections of virtue, they warred on the bosses and the interests, on the apathetic citizen, and also on the loyal citizen who was afraid that a reform movement would give his city a bad name.

In a few cities, such as New York in 1895, reform scored famous victories, but they rarely lasted. A kind of bitter comedy followed. A few months after the victory over Tammany and police graft, the moral temperature of the city dropped appreciably, as any politician could have foreseen. The amateurs began to squabble among themselves.

The machine professionals took over once again. The new mayor, William F. Strong, was so embittered by his one term that he vowed never again to offer himself for public service. All in all, the ups and downs of most morally fired reform campaigns bore out Mr. Dooley's claim that it was easier and more rational to train lobsters to fly than it was to turn men into angels by means of the ballot box.

. . .

For our time of urban violence and bafflement the moral reformers do not have much to offer. But there is something—not answers perhaps, but impetus—to be got from another school of reformers. . . .

Among these reformers were Mayor Samuel M. ("Golden Rule") Jones of Toledo . . . ; his successor Brand Whitlock, who had been brought into politics by the fiery John Peter Altgeld;* and in Cleveland, Mayor Tom L. Johnson. . . .

These men accepted the realities of politics, but they also celebrated the possibilities of the city. . . . Their creed was summed up in the title of one of Howe's* books, *The City: The Hope of Democracy.* . . . They believed that it was possible, and necessary, for the city to become not only a place of justice and honesty but also an agency in unprecedented social service for all the people.

John Peter Altgeld (1847–1902)—reform governor of Illinois.

Frederic C. Howe (1867–1940)—American lawyer and political scientist.

In this famous book the author exposed the corruption that existed in most large cities of the nation. Steffens was one of a group of writers whom President Theodore Roosevelt called "muckrakers" because they raked up the dirt about American society. It was the hope of the muckrakers that publicity and exposure would bring about reform.

2

Pittsburgh: A City Ashamed

by LINCOLN STEFFENS

MINNEAPOLIS was an example of police corruption; St. Louis, of financial corruption; Pittsburgh is an example of both police and financial corruption. The two other cities each have found an official who has exposed them. Pittsburgh has had no such man and no exposure. The city has been described physically as "hell with the lid off"; politically it is hell with the lid on. I am not going to lift the lid. The expo-

From *The Shame of the Cities*, by Lincoln Steffens. Reprinted by permission of Doubleday & Company, Inc.

sitions of what the people know and stand is the purpose of these articles, not the exposure of corruption, and the exposure of Pittsburgh is not necessary. There are earnest men in the town who declare it must blow up of itself soon. I doubt that, but even if it does burst, the people of Pittsburgh will learn little more than they know now. It is not ignorance that keeps American citizens subservient, neither is it indifference. The Pittsburghers know, and a strong minority of them care; they have risen against their ring and beaten it, only to look about and find another ring around them. Angry and ashamed, Pittsburgh is a type of city that has tried to be free and failed.

A sturdy city it is, too, the second in Pennsylvania. Two rivers flow past it to make a third, the Ohio, in front, and all around and beneath it are natural gas and coal which feed a thousand furnaces that smoke all day and flame all night to make Pittsburgh the Birmingham of America. Rich in natural resources, it is richest in the quality of its population. Six days and six nights these people labor, molding iron and forging steel, and they are not tired; on the seventh day they rest, because that is the Sabbath. They are Scotch Presbyterians and Protestant Irish. This stock had an actual majority not many years ago, and now, though the population has grown to 354,000 in Pittsburgh proper . . . the Scotch and Scotch-Irish still predominate, and their clean, strong faces characterize the crowds in the streets. Canny, busy, and brave, they built up their city almost in secret, making millions and hardly mentioning it. Not till outsiders came in to buy some of them out did the world (and Pittsburgh and some of the millionaires in it) discover that the Iron City had been making not only steel and glass, but multi-

Pittsburgh's steel mills run day and night creating steady employment for many and millions of dollars for a few. (Fritz Henle, Monkmeyer)

millionaires. A banker told a businessman as a secret one day about three years ago that within six months a "bunch of about a hundred new millionaires would be born in Pittsburgh," and the births happened on time. And more beside. But even the bloom of millions did not hurt the city. Pittsburgh is an unpretentious, prosperous city of tremendous industry and healthy, steady men.

Superior as it is in some other respects, however, Scotch-Irish Pittsburgh, politically, is no better than Irish New York or Scandinavian Minneapolis, and little better than German St. Louis. These people, like any other strain of free American, have despoiled the government—despoiled it, let it be despoiled, and bowed to the despoiling boss. There is nothing in the un-American excuse that this or that foreign nationality has prostituted "our great and glorious institutions." We all do it, all breeds alike. And there is nothing in the complaint that the lower elements of our city populations are the source of our disgrace. In St. Louis corruption came from the top, in Minneapolis from the bottom. In Pittsburgh it comes from both extremities, but it began above.

Here, the author, a noted newspaperman specializing in urban problems, tries to explain how New Yorkers feel about their government and why they feel that way. While most people boast about their city, New Yorkers complain about theirs.

3

What Have You Done for Me Lately?: The Ins and Outs of New York City Politics

by WARREN MOSCOW

NEW YORK'S politicians and officeholders operate in a political climate that is as demanding and confusing as anything outside of Washington, D.C. Part of this comes from the voter whose attitude toward the city's political system is akin to that of the jealous

From *What Have You Done for Me Lately?: The Ins and Outs of New York City Politics,* by Warren Moscow (Englewood Cliffs, N.J.: Prentice-Hall, Inc., 1967), pp. 230–34. Copyright © 1967 by Warren Moscow. Reprinted by permission of McIntosh and Otis, Inc.

It is true New Yorkers are constantly tripping over construction. But construction of commercial buildings and luxury apartments does not solve the serious housing problem that threatens to evict the lower- and middle-income families from Manhattan altogether. (UPI)

wife who always hopes for the best and fears for the worst. In loose conversation, the voter is certain that all politicians and officeholders are crooked, yet he will exculpate, when pressed, each and every one familiar to him. He resents special privileges—for others. . . . He gripes daily about the rush-hour crowds in the subway, and wonders why someone hasn't arranged to stagger the working hours for people in other occupations. He thinks sincerely that the city is going to pot and not even the new building construction, over which he has been tripping constantly for years, can convince him otherwise. He thinks the city is dirty, compared with others he has visited or heard of, but doesn't connect that with the cigarette butt that he invariably tosses into the street.

.   .   .

It has more to commend it than its skyline, its theaters, stores, and museums, its crowds and its worldliness. . . .

There is no city that rivals New York in overall services—such things as the frequency of garbage collection, the twenty-four-hour transit system, housing efforts, concern over the safety of the elevators —which make New York possible—fire-fighting and emergency equipment.

In all these and countless others, New York's superior standards and efforts are hidden by the immensity of the problems created by the city's density, the fight for space in the heart of the city. Take traffic. It is a cinch to keep traffic flowing smoothly through the main streets of a city that boasts of possibly one thirty-story "tower" dominating the four-story buildings that make up the rest of its business district. That represents no density problem at all.

But in New York the forty-story buildings, which are as commonplace as the four-story structures elsewhere, attract at least ten times as many pedestrians, autos, taxis, service trucks, and delivery vans as the four-story buildings with the equivalent street frontage. . . . The fact that New York's streets year after year handle a steadily increasing flow, and still are choked no worse than in the days of the horse-drawn van, is a tribute to the effort that has been put into traffic direction and control. Yet the citizen grumbles that the problem has not yet been solved.

Then there is water supply. A century or more ago the city reached out beyond its own boundaries for new and better sources after its own shallow wells were no longer adequate. The Hudson is tidal and salty for sixty miles north, so New York first tapped the Croton River in Westchester, then bought up half of Putnam County for reservoirs for both storage and supply. Later it tunneled under the increasingly polluted Hudson to bring water from the Catskills and finally it stretched out to the headwaters of the Delaware. All of the territory it included in its watershed received the guarantee that the city would forever protect the source of supply against pollution; it would furnish the locality water from the reservoirs it built and would charge no more for that water than it charged its own citizens. In the case of the cities along the Delaware in three other states, it guaranteed to keep the Delaware flowing for them, in summer drought, by releasing from its reservoirs the spring flood-waters it stored annually. It produced the best water in America from the point of view of purity and taste, and it also furnished the most, meeting a peak demand of 1,200,000,000 gallons a day.

It was a marvelous achievement, accepted by the

The top photo shows the Ashokan Reservoir in Ulster County, New York, during a drought. Below is the same reservoir after sufficient rainfall has filled it. (Wide World)

citizenry without comment. Then came a drought that in 1966 had lasted for five years and affected the entire Northeast. . . .

It seemed to some that the city administration should have pointed with pride to its water accomplishments; should have boasted that the city still had water despite the unprecedented drought, while other cities were at the crisis stage; that there was nothing wrong with New York's water planning that a single year of normal rainfall couldn't straighten out. The administration—with a base in sad experience—felt that the public would never accept the accomplishments of the previous decade or the previous century as an excuse for the shortage of the moment. They quoted, as politicians are prone to do with a momentous ritualism, the hypothetical story of the constituent and the politician who chided him for ingratitude.

The voter, according to the story, acknowledged all past favors and added, "But what have you done for me lately?"

How to attract able men for service in city government has been an age-old problem. In ancient Athens all citizens were required to serve. Once in service, how to keep men efficient and incorruptible is a greater problem still. In this selection the author explains the difficulty of making men in city government thoroughly honest.

4

How to Keep Them from Taking a Buck

by RICHARD REEVES

SOMEWHERE in Dayton, Ohio, there is a dishonest man. The same thing could be said of Jersey City. Both of these cities have populations of almost 300,000 and history books don't have any examples of that many getting together in one place without a single dishonest man among them.

New York City has more workers on its payroll than Dayton or Jersey City has people. In fact, only 40 American cities have populations greater than 312,000, which is the number of people working for New York City. So it should come as no great shock that some New York civil servants are on the take.

Stories of municipal employees accused of taking, and respectable citizens accused of giving, have dominated the local news since . . . James L. Marcus, former Commissioner of Water Supply, Gas and Electricity, was charged with taking a $16,000 kickback on a reservoir-cleaning contract.

There are now at least 13 investigations of municipal corruption being conducted by five agencies. . . .

The news . . . included several corruption stories: The Police Department announced that 10 policemen were to face charges that they got some of the money collected from 147 East Side businesses named on a detective's purported payoff or gift list; a milk company president was arrested and four Health Department inspectors face departmental payoff charges because of Mr. Hogan's* inquiry into the milk industry; Mr. Koota* began investigating a Human Resources job-training contract, and a chemical company executive was indicted for refusing to talk about alleged gifts to city employees.

Was the city being stolen from under us during the reform administration of John V. Lindsay? No, not really. Many of the investigations centered on heavy graft—payoffs to police and inspectors—that was going on long before Mr. Lindsay became May-

Hogan and *Koota*—district attorneys of New York City and Brooklyn.

or. The investigators themselves say that city departments are always being studied—on the theory that there has to be a dishonest man in Dayton—and that the publicity surrounding the investigations has encouraged usually silent New Yorkers to file new complaints about graft.

New York, contrary to legend, is not that bad, according to Wallace S. Sayre and Herbert Kaufman, the authors of *Governing New York City*.

"Those exposés have happened often enough," they wrote in their massive study of city government, "to give wide circulation to the notion that the government and politics of New York City hold high rank, if not the highest place, among American cities in the art and practice of official corruption. Actually, this impression is largely the result of the city's system to ferret out and give great and dramatic publicity to violations of the rules. The system might properly claim first rank among American cities in the art and practice of exposing corruption."

The number of local investigating agencies—New York, for example, has five district attorneys—and competition between those agencies is one of the reasons for continuous exposure of official wrongdoing.

The current crowd of investigations should have a healthy effect, according to the investigators. "After this, a city employee is going to think a long time before he takes a buck," said a high official in one of the probing agencies. ". . . And even more important, a lot of citizens will have the guts to report anyone who asks them for anything."

The author of this selection does not deny that the nation's cities need federal and state funds. But federal and state funding alone, he believes, will not solve America's urban crisis. He suggests we make some far-reaching changes in the structure of local government and in the quality and quantity of manpower that supplies city services.

5

Beyond the Machine

by EDWARD N. COSTIKYAN

Why are the mayors all quitting?
Why are the cities all broke?
Why are the people all angry?
Why are we dying of smoke?
Why are the streets unprotected?
Why are the schools in distress?
Why is the trash uncollected?
How did we make such a mess?

—ANON.

From "Cities Can Work," by Edward N. Costikyan, *Saturday Review*, April 4, 1970, pp. 19–21. Copyright © 1970 by Saturday Review, Inc. Reprinted by permission of the author.

"Then the question is: Do we want a prosperity based on increased government spending or a prosperity based on cutting government expenses? That's where I begin not to follow."

(Drawing by Alan Dunn. Copyright © 1964 by The New Yorker Magazine, Inc.)

THIS bit of verse sums up with commendable clarity and directness the problems of the cities as we enter a new decade. The answers are less clear, and the solutions still more obscure. . . . The nearly universal prescription would have the federal government provide massive financial assistance and take over as many city governmental functions as can possibly be palmed off upwards. . . .

Although some of a city's programs, such as welfare, properly are financed in whole, instead of only in part, by the federal government, massive increases in federal aid would *not* solve a city's problems, but rather would be quickly absorbed by the money-consuming monster that city government can become. Therefore, the causes of the crises within our cities demand a different type of federal help for two reasons: The predominant cause of city crises is the collapse and destruction of the political machine. The second cause is the shortage of a supply of cheap labor essential to the growth and life of any city. . . .

The base of the machine was the captain of the election district or precinct. He was in charge of a one-to-two-block area for the party. And he was in charge year round. If a resident had a problem—leaking ceilings, no water or heat, a son in trouble with the law, a shortage of cash or food—he turned to his neighbor the captain. The captain, if he himself could not deal with the problem, took the constituent to "the leader" at the local clubhouse. There the problem was explained, and the leader undertook to solve it by contacting someone in the bureaucracy who was beholden to the leader.

This power of lateral invasion into the bureaucracy made efficient administration of a large city possible. It kept the bureaucracy hopping. But it also encouraged corruption. The average citizen, however, was willing to tolerate a degree of corruption as the price of his having ready access to government services. But the more affluent members of society (the backbone of every reform movement), seeing in this lateral access to government services (and not needing those services) potential and actual corruption, set out to destroy that access and the system that produced it. . . .

The reform answer to the machine as the personnel pool for government was the creation of a competing source of manpower: civil service. . . . But with the collapse of the machine, civil service

The New York Uniformed Sanitationmen's Association (garbagemen) went out on strike—and stayed out as the city slowly subsided into a mounting mountain of offal. (Pat Oliphant, The Denver Post)

has monopolized the field, and the administrative results have been disastrous, for the bureaucracies have a double layer of protection that deprives any elected official of the power to get the bureaucrats to do their jobs. One layer is the impossibility of firing a civil servant. The other is the civil service unions, which have such power over the city—in the absence of alternative sources of manpower—that in the final analysis the bureaucracies are in a position to dictate to elected officials and their appointees. . . .

The destruction of the political machine has left the unionized civil service bureaucracies with the same control over the life of the city that the machine once enjoyed and abused sufficiently to lead to the growth of civil service.

Finally, the destruction of the machine has left some governmental functions without anyone to perform them. The city's election machinery, for example, was once operated by the political parties. The parties, rather than the city, not only trained the election inspectors but paid them (the city paid a pittance, and still does, but the parties no longer can transform this pittance into reasonable compensation). The parties saw that the polls were open when they should be, and that the voting machines worked. True, the parties sometimes abused their power. . . .

The solution to all this is not the recreation of the political machine, an impossible task given the level of competence of their present leaders and personnel. Rather it is to stimulate alternative methods of performing the necessary governmental and political functions that the machines once performed. On the governmental level, the first task is to create a device to perform the function once provided by the machine of giving the citizen direct lateral access to his government. The most popular proposal to accomplish this has been called decentralization. I prefer to call it reallocation of government functions. The proposal is that each government function will be assigned to the lowest and smallest governmental entity qualified to perform it. Under this approach, basic government services, such as police patrolling, street cleaning, and parking and housing enforcement, will be overseen by a local administrator in charge of a district of about 100,000 people. Other services, such as those dealing with air and water pollution, would be administered on a regional basis. In between, city or county governments would perform those functions they are best capable of.

But essential to the proposal is the notion that the

local administrator be elected by and be responsible
to the voters whose streets he is supposed to keep
clean and safe, that the existing civil service bureaucracies be eliminated, that their functions and personnel be reassigned to the appropriate level of
government—local, city, county, or regional—and
that the elected administrator of each level of government be given substantially greater power over
those he supervises than city officials now have over
unionized civil servants, who also possess a fair
amount of political power. . . .

It is hoped that this reallocation of government
functions will achieve a number of salutary effects:

- humanizing the presently unpersonal government
  furnished by most cities to their citizenry;

- eliminating the bureaucratic rigidity and waste
  of manpower that have characterized increasingly centralized city government;

- placing responsibility for city government on
  identifiable individuals subject to popular control and, when appropriate, the removal from
  office by those they are supposed to be serving;

- reducing the cost of government by eliminating
  the layers of administrators, which result, for
  example, in less than 10 percent of the New
  York City Police Department's personnel (and
  analogous percentages in the other departments)
  performing line duty. . . .

On the city governmental level, there is a tremendous need for short-term, vigorous, young manpower to deal with the emergencies that every city
constantly faces and the special emergencies it faces
from time to time. The city's existing manpower can-

not meet or effectively deal with these emergencies. . . .

The answer to all these situations is a special emergency force, consisting of young men and women who would devote two to three years of their lives to serving their city just as they are now asked to serve their country. They could quickly be given sufficient knowledge of city government to spot housing violations and to file complaints. They could move into a problem area, take it over house by house, and clean it up. They could provide extra police protection in high crime areas; collect garbage, if that were necessary; arrest narcotics pushers (which would be necessary); and bring help and guidance to the oppressed city dwellers who live in degradation. They could collect the rents and make the repairs the absent landlords refused to make. Some could first complete their educations and then bring medical and legal services to the people and places that need them. No picnic, it would be hard and sometimes dangerous work. What mayor would not rejoice at such an emergency force? . . .

Federal sponsorship of such a program, including financial help and especially exemption from the draft, would do more to revitalize our cities than any big gobs of money we are likely to see from Washington. . . .

The cities also need a federal yardstick program to build housing at rational costs. If industry and labor cannot do the job—and they simply cannot, given today's costs—let the federal government do what it did in the South in the 1930's: unabashedly go into the business of doing what the private sector cannot do. . . .

The cost of building housing is the same as the cost of building commercial structures, but the returns on the commercial structure are many times higher. Small wonder that housing construction has stopped and private financing for housing has dried up, while new office buildings spring up one after another.

We need a federal yardstick operation with self-renewing federal money, and if necessary, the creation of a new housing construction work force to build the millions of dwellings the cities will need in the coming years. The creation of such a housing work force might well go a long way toward solving the impasse between the black man and the existing construction unions. There is no stimulus like competition, or even the threat of it, to produce action where action is needed. . . .

Our cities will survive and be governable only if those we elect have effective power over those who are supposed to do the work, only if those we elect are responsible and accountable to the people who elect them, and only if the federal government gives the kind of help that will make manpower available to do the work that survival requires.

The day the police went on strike in Montreal, Canada, two men were slain and forty-eight people were wounded or injured in rioting, bank holdups, and robberies. When firemen went on strike in Gary, Indiana, buildings burned to the ground. When sanitation men went on strike in New York City the garbage piled so high that the health department feared the spread of disease. What does this mean for the public?

6

Revolt of the Civil Servants

by A. H. RASKIN

ALL the fears, frustrations, and furies of the nation's decaying cities beat down on the civil service. The policeman, once a symbol of authority with small boys tagging respectfully in his wake eager to touch the magic blue cloth, finds himself dodging sniper's bullets or being spat upon as a "pig." The fireman,

From "Revolt of the Civil Servants," by A. H. Raskin, *Saturday Review*, December 7, 1968, pp. 27–30. Copyright © 1968 by Saturday Review, Inc. Reprinted by permission of the author.

(Joe Molnar)

AGAINST
RACIST TEACHERS
EXTRA TIME
COPS 'N SCHOOLS

WAR & FASCISM

(Joe Molnar)

responding to alarms in the ghetto, is peppered with
bricks and bottles as he prepares to risk his life
to save someone else's. The teacher, already dis-
mayed by the bars to learning created by poverty,
family disintegration, and the general hopelessness of
inherited dependency, must also wrestle with the new
pressures born of the Negro's struggle for more self-
rule.

In every other phase of municipal service, from
welfare through garbage collection, the woes of the
cities make each day's duties a challenge—and usually a misery—for those who work for the cities. Little
wonder then that, in a period of widespread rebellion
against established institutions, the discontents of
public employees are erupting in illegal strikes, slow-
downs, and other forms of revolt against that stuffi-
est and most bureaucratic of all institutions—the
government that public employees are sworn to
uphold.

At every level of government—federal, state, and
local—civil service strikes are just as illegal today
as they were in 1919 when Calvin Coolidge, then
governor of Massachusetts, backed the firing of
Boston police strikers with the declaration that
"there is no right to strike against the public safety
by anybody, anywhere, any time." Yet New York
City has had almost three years of what amounts
to a nonstop crisis involving strikes and strike threats
by teachers, subway workers, nurses, doctors, policemen, firemen, sanitation men, welfare workers, and
employees of other vital agencies.

So successful have the New York unions been in
enshrining the principle that unlawful strikes pay off
in fatter wage agreements and a larger union voice
in basic policy decisions, that the virus has spread
to cities all over the United States.

STRIKES BY PUBLIC EMPLOYEES

Employees in Civil Service	1968	1969
Federal government	2,737,000	2,757,000
State/local government	9,109,000	9,469,000
Total government employees	11,846,000	12,226,000
Total civilian work force	78,737,000	80,733,000
Government employment as percentage of total force	15%	15%

Work Stoppages: State and Local Government Employees	1967	1969
Total work stoppages	181	[1]411
Number of workers involved	132,000	[1]160,000
Number of man-days idle	1,250,000	[1]745,700

---

[1] Includes 2 stoppages of Federal employees, affecting 600 workers and resulting in 1,100 man-days of idleness.

(U.S. Department of Labor, Bureau of Labor Statistics)

"...the newspapers, the TV networks, the railroads, farmers, schoolteachers, truckers, firemen, policemen—in fact, gentlemen, the whole damn <u>world</u> is deadlocked on the wage issue. I never thought it would end this way."

(Drawing by Alan Dunn. Copyright © 1967 by The New Yorker Magazine, Inc.)

.   .   .

New York State . . . has a law that makes it unnecessary to strike for union recognition or grievance machinery. The Empire State's Taylor Law, based on the recommendations of five nationally prominent experts in peaceful labor management relations, is designed to give civil service unions every possible assurance that their public employer will not be able to hide behind the strike ban to deny them the wages and other benefits that fairness requires. Not only does the law oblige state and local agencies to sign written contracts with the union representing their workers, but it also provides for impartial fact-finding to break deadlocks over what constitutes a fair settlement. The whole aim is to stop strikes by removing any valid basis for striking.

In some respects, New York City has gone even further than the state to achieve the same goal. The

Lindsay administration joined with most of the city's civil service unions two years ago in setting up an Office of Collective Bargaining (OCB) to promote labor harmony by providing for neutral peace proposals in all contract disputes. The unions have an equal say with the city in every phase of the agency's operation, and George Meany, president of the AFL-CIO, has hailed it as a national model.

But the New York sanitation union refused ever to get under the OCB umbrella. Its leaders felt they could get more for their 10,000 members by staying out and then demanding richer contracts than anyone else got. This approach is familiar enough in general union practice, but it has two main defects in the civil service.

One is that it represents a prescription for municipal bankruptcy because the ninety other unions New York deals with won't stand still for such one-upmanship; the result is an endless leapfrog in which every union tries to climb over the backs of all the others, precisely the disease the OCB was intended to cure.

· · ·

When it came time in the fall for the city to negotiate new agreements with all its uniformed forces, Lindsay was obliged for the first time to grapple with the reality of illegal strike threats by policemen and firemen as well as the still seething sanitation men. . . .

This three-way rivalry was the last thing Lindsay needed. The city was already being torn apart by the most divisive strike in its history—the walkout of 55,000 unionized teachers in a battle that quickly moved beyond its stated goal of due process in teacher tenure to a confrontation between New

York's black and white communities on the explosive issue of school desegregation.

. . .

What conclusions flow from all this on either the correctness or the practicality of trying to sustain the age-old doctrine that there is no right to strike against the government? My own conviction is that the basic ban, for all the imperfections of its observance, is essential to orderly government.

. . .

The real justification for maintaining inviolate the legal ban on public strikes lies in the nature of government as the embodiment of all the people. It is not a business organized for profit; it cannot move away; it cannot lock out its employees. The conventional notion of strikes as tests of strength in which the pressures of the marketplace operate to constrain both management and union simply does not apply. For that reason, a strike against government becomes an interference with the political process, an effort by one segment of the people to misuse its control over a specific service as a weapon with which to bludgeon the entire community into submission.

. . .

Valid as many of the proposed policy changes may be, questions of this kind should not be resolved under the gun of a strike. Otherwise elected officials will become captives of embattled civil servants, responding to coercion, not persuasion.

. . .

At no time have the police been subject to so much criticism as they are today. Trained to apprehend the hardened criminal, they are less inclined to be sensitive to the so-called nonviolent student protester who violates the law because he feels he must if he is to reform American society. What distinction can be made between the thief who violates the law by stealing and the student who in anger and in protest destroys property?

7

Policing the Police

by HALLOCK HOFFMAN

. . . MORE and more Americans, white and black, have come to look on policemen as potential enemies. More and more policemen have come to feel that they work in hostile territory, surrounded by citizens on whom they dare not count for neutrality, let alone support. Efforts by policemen to do their

From "Policing the Police," by Hallock Hoffman, *The Center Magazine*, May 1968, Vol. II, No. 4, a publication of the Center for the Study of Democratic Institutions in Santa Barbara, California. Reprinted by permission.

jobs, as they understand them, precipitate riots; efforts by citizens to express opposition to public policies bring them too often under police violence. We have to ask whether the warfare between the citizens and the police results from the "system"—from the whole social arrangement of our society, of which the police are a part—or whether it is something that may be ameliorated by reforms of police regulations, training, recruiting, and administration.

It is worth recalling that the policing of a community is part of larger systems, and the way these larger systems perform influences policing. For example, what policemen do is directly related to the operation of courts and to prosecuting and defense attorneys. It is also directly dependent on the law and legislation. It is less directly but closely related to the operation of the jails and penitentiaries and the probation system. It is related, though more distantly, to the politics of municipal administration; and at one further remove to national welfare programs. . . .

Policemen and their professional associations constantly lobby in state and national legislatures for harsher penalties for drug abuse, and for an increased number of drugs and drug uses to be made illegal. It would seem to follow that when they succeed in getting another drug labeled as dangerous, and its use or possession labeled "criminal," they are making their own work harder—more acts are now crimes, and more people criminals. But the more crimes and criminals, the more need for policemen. Steady growth of bureaucratic administration is a feature of all governmental departments. It occurs as "need" is "demonstrated." The way police departments demonstrate the need for growth and strength, rank and power, is through increases in crime and criminals.

This factor has something to do also with the growth of crime statistics. The more the records improve and the reporting of crimes already on the books increases, the more crime can be seen. Police departments use as internal measures of efficiency and value—and also to persuade outsiders, like legislators and city councils and other appropriating agencies—the rate in which the department "clears" crimes that have been counted. Only those crimes listed (that is, only those which are counted by the police statistics system) have to be cleared; once a crime is listed, it can be cleared only by an arrest or by arrest-and-conviction. (Which crimes get listed and which do not tells quite a bit about the operation of police departments.) There is a tendency for the crimes that are easily cleared to be increased faster than those which are harder to clear. For example, the possession, use, or sale of marijuana does not get listed *unless* a criminal is apprehended committing it; a marijuana arrest is tantamount to a crime listed *and* cleared simultaneously, and helps any department's "averages." (The "per cent of crimes cleared" is the measure used by the FBI in the uniform crime reports each year.) On the other hand, a robbery has to be listed whenever the owner of the property claims effectively that he has been robbed; and listing a robbery lays on the police department a necessity to clear off a mark otherwise standing against it on its records.

A further reason for the police to want harsher penalties is their common practice of "trading" lighter sentences for heavier ones to persuade "criminals" already caught to help catch additional criminals, or to get guilty pleas. When a prosecutor tries a case,

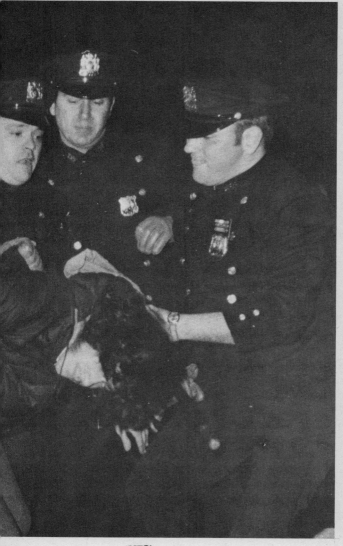

(UPI)

there is always a danger he may lose it; when the
prosecutor and the defense attorney can agree on a
guilty plea, the prosecutor has a sure case, and the
police a sure clearance; hence, a variety of available
"serious" charges creates a basis for trading down
from possible conviction on severe charges to guilty
pleas on lesser charges. Policemen use the same
process to acquire informers; the more varied and
extensive the catalogue of "crimes," the greater the
opportunity for the arresting officer to award a
lighter charge in exchange for information.

Policemen are agents for maintaining external
order. Most policemen take their cues from dominant
members in their communities, i.e., businessmen and
the generally influential. The evidence of good police
work, in the eyes of such policemen, is that no property is being damaged, and the people who count
are not being hurt. To achieve this result, the policeman seeks signs of incipient violence to persons and
property *before* the violence begins. He does this by
looking for anything out of the ordinary—he is suspicious of the unusual, the out-of-the-way, and the
extraordinary.

This makes the policeman enforce the community
"mores" as well as its laws. Indeed, if he has to
choose between mores and laws, he usually chooses
the former. Long hair, unusual though harmless be-
havior, peculiar dress, or "minority" color are all
signs that attract his attention, because he believes
differences of these kinds are likely to lead to conflict
and violence. . . . The policeman identifies his work
and his interests with those of the owners or con-
trollers of property. They are usually the dominant
persons in his community. They can cause him
trouble, and get him advantage. This is only to
say that the policeman fits into the American class

system. In general, he is a lower-middle-class person; and his aspiring upward mobility appears to him to depend upon pleasing the upper-middle-class people for whom, in the main, he works.

Because of this identification, many ghetto crimes against persons are tolerantly dismissed by policemen as "that's the way *they* are," while damage of the ghetto property of non-ghetto landlords is treated as grave disorder. Another result is that young people who look like solid white middle-class youths, especially when properly washed and barbered, will be judged as engaged in high jinks and pranks when they break windows or invade dormitories, while minor damage caused by ghetto or hippie youths will be viewed as criminal. "Unusual" youths are a visible threat to the social order, according to many middle-class parents and school administrators and policemen; the policeman becomes the agent of the parents and the schools in seeking to make the young conform to the accepted pattern.

These examples are a long way from the guerrilla warfare of our cities, but I believe they are connected. They show why the cry of "law and order" in the mouth of the policeman and of those who want to "support" him sounds so threatening to liberty. Liberty is not restrained unless it is claimed for actions that are different from those the dominant group in the society approves. The identification of the police with dominant middle-class majority opinions, beliefs, and mores threatens the freedom and safety of all those who do not fit the middle-class model. The threat by police, in the name of order, becomes critical when those who are different become visible, when they attract attention, as, lately, they are increasingly doing.

(Wide World)

The root of all the problems, as the National Commission proclaimed, is white racism. But we have had white racism for a long time. The new circumstance is that black people, proud of being black, are beginning to assert the rightness and value of their "differences" and demanding what the Constitution and the political leaders have been promising them. Black people have come to see that they really could have what they think they deserve; they are being denied not because white society cannot provide but because it won't. The frustration the Commission describes in terms of millions of missing jobs, homes, and welfare arrangements is not necessary. Suffering that is neither necessary nor just is unbearable.

But the forces of segregation and ostracism and economic deprivation have crammed minority populations into crowded and circumscribed areas of the major cities. They have made these areas explosive; they have also made the areas—from a police point of view—enclaves within which misbehavior and violence may be confined. The police have armed themselves for battle. They intend to keep the campaigns localized.

Though not yet as acute, the problem of the peace protesters is also becoming dangerous. The young are deeply involved as the Vietnam war sets the stage for general drop-out. Their life-style, including their interest in drugs (which is reminiscent of their fathers' and mothers' flirtations with alcohol at a comparable age) and in fashions of their own, singles them out for police attention. Their parents are frightened of them; the police are licensed to use force to control them; and the political situation seems to leaders in office so to endanger our national survival as to warrant strong measures to keep dissent in check. This creates the second big potential

explosion. That it and the black rebellion may co-
alesce in the radical politics . . . is certainly a possibility.

How can the policemen of our larger cities be
equipped to meet these potential calamities? The
easy answer, the one being given, is that they should
have all the technically sophisticated arms now available in order to fight a major war—the kinds of
arms that stun and sicken and incapacitate, rather
than kill. . . .

Another kind of equipment would be possible. It
would depend less on arms and more on moral power
and better training and new policies.

[1] Police departments could recruit large numbers
of young men and women from among the deprived,
and deploy them to protect each other and the ghettos. The point of this is to eliminate the archaic
concepts of who and what makes a suitable policeman, and who or what is to be protected. Self-deter-
mination requires self-policing.

[2] The police could be trained in non-violence, and
relieved of guns in connection with riot control. So
far, guns have only started or escalated violence—
they have not suppressed it.

[3] Police could be specialized. Most of the center-
city battles have been set off by arrests for minor
offenses, including traffic offenses. Although policemen either ridicule or detest the idea, it is possible
to think of making specialists out of police personnel, many of whom might thus never be expected to
deal with "dangerous criminals." They could have
distinctive uniforms (and would be known by all
to be non-threatening), play helpful rather than
purely disciplinary roles, and, most important, be
rewarded for such helpfulness rather than for tough-

ness and bravery. Police bravery causes more troubles than it corrects: we ought to have specialists in that, too, who would concentrate on making bravery useful.

[4] A variety of lesser notions may be suggested: Every time a policeman draws his gun, he should be obliged to fill out a complete report that would be submitted to an administrative committee and filed among his permanent personnel records. Police should be trained to shoot below the knees, rather than, as now, to shoot through the heart. . . . Some policemen should be commissioned to buy or rent residences in troublesome districts and to become "neighborhood constables" there. They would aim to become integrated members of the community rather than to exist as "the authority." They would not replace other specialists—patrols in cars, detectives, narcotics agents, etc.—but would give local residents police support against those who take advantage of them. . . . Police departments ought to be decentralized, both in operation and in control. They are now run like occupying armies; they ought to be run like a chain of service stations. . . . Communities should be encouraged to develop committees of oversight to see that the police are doing their jobs well. Such civilian oversight could do much to reduce the feeling that the police are brutal and abrasive—if they are not. . . . Crowd- and riot-control squads could be specially trained, and policemen without this training should not be assigned to such work.

· · ·

If we can keep an experimental turn of mind, and aim at de-escalating violence rather than at containing or preventing conflict (which we neither can nor should try to stop) we will get to community-police relations that work. It will take serious and thoughtful attention from everybody—police departments, municipal, state, and national administrations, and all citizens—to get through the coming crisis without disastrous damage to democratic institutions.

In this selection the author describes the working day of the man who occupies the second hardest job in the nation. If the first most difficult job is that of the President of the United States, the second is Mayor of New York City. Born to wealth and privilege, Mayor John Lindsay has succeeded, where others have failed, in appealing to the city's racial minorities. Like Carl Stokes of Cleveland (see Reading #9), when Mayor Lindsay tells the people of the ghetto to "cool it," they listen.

8

Mayor in Motion— New York's Lindsay: Gung-Ho Guy in a Brutal Job

by JIM FLAGLER

.   .   .

OF ALL the political prizes for which men struggle in this land, the office of the Mayor of the City of New York is the most dubiously rewarding. As the bromide goes, it's a dead end; of 102 previous mayors, only a couple, before this century, have risen to

From "Mayor in Motion—New York's Lindsay: Gung-Ho Guy in a Brutal Job," by Jim Flagler, *Look* Magazine, June 24, 1969. Copyright © 1969 by Cowles Communications, Inc. Reprinted by permission of the Editors of *Look* Magazine.

New York's Mayor Lindsay enjoys identifying with today's youth. Here he is seen with members of the Urban Fellowship Program, a government trainee program much like the student teachers program.

higher elective status. The mayor must take the blame for policies made elsewhere, usually at the state capitol in Albany, and for the inertia or skull-duggery of an impacted bureaucracy of 300,000. Even in a nonelection year, the office is brutally demanding—"the second most impossible job," it has been endlessly said, after the Presidency.

Upon arising in Gracie Mansion, the barny, 170-year-old frame house and former museum that serves as the official residence, a New York mayor is fittingly greeted by a view of Hell Gate, a turbulent passage of the East River's polluted waters. Lindsay customarily gets to work before 8 A.M., either at an office in the Mansion or in City Hall, another of New York's few unrazed pieces of early Americana. Until he retires 16 hours later, he rarely has an inactive moment or a private one.

To grasp the dimensions of Lindsay's workdays, consider his concerns over one 96-hour span. The Mayor was called upon to chair important meetings with a delegation of the Citizens Committee of 100 to save Harlem Hospital, with a panel of his top police brass, with his official "cabinet," and with George Romney, the U.S. Secretary of Housing and Urban Development, and a group of city-housing experts. He received, with varying degrees of ceremony, courtesy calls from an Israeli general, the U.S. Secretary of Labor, and the Australian Minister of Social Welfare and of Aboriginal Affairs, as well as from visiting fellow mayors of Detroit, Montreal and Phoenix. He had to lend the official presence to a street-corner 75th-birthday celebration of the Motion Picture Association of America, a New York Mets booster dinner, a Warsaw Ghetto Commemoration Day proclamation, and the start of the "Lock It and Pocket the Key" campaign, aimed at cutting down the city's present annual rate of 100,000 car thefts.

Formal speechmaking engagements took the Mayor to a Baptist ministers' convocation in a Harlem church, a Convention and Visitors Bureau luncheon, a Fordham University lecture platform, an American Arbitration Association dinner and a black-tie centennial celebration at the American Museum of Natural History. For purely political purposes, Lindsay showed up at a small homeowners' beer-and-sandwich party in unfriendly Queens, an afternoon kaffeeklatsch in a Bronx living room and a midtown Manhattan street rally to open Lindsay campaign headquarters. In addition to being dogged continuously by a magazine writer, he held a televised press conference and granted individual interviews to a Washington correspondent of *The New York Times,* a Detroit *Free Press* reporter and a girl journalism student. An unexpected supplicant was the Israeli consul, agitated by the burning of his country's flag outside the consulate, supposedly by local members of Fatah, the Arab terrorist group. (The Mayor identified the ringleader as a once-deported troublemaker and got on the phone to U.S. Immigration officials to urge another speedy exit.) In the course of these activities, Lindsay had to express himself publicly on a bewildering variety of subjects—antiballistic missiles, school breakfasts, a "fourth platoon" duty shift for policemen, the urban policies of the Nixon Administration, the proposed narrowing of a traffic island on an outlying boulevard, rent controls and a report by a Soviet newspaper that Russian United Nations employees were being mugged in New York like everybody else.

.   .   .

One of the most demanding aspects of Lindsay's job is talk. In fact, the mayoral mouth is seldom allowed to close. Between scheduled events and visitors, Lindsay keeps right on talking, save for when he's listening. Politics is the sum of mumbled minutiae, and there is always an aide or tactician ready to grab the Mayor's ear and talk over details. Lindsay claims—with demonstrable accuracy—that he is able to concentrate on two things at once. It is not unusual for him, as he is whisked from one engagement to another in his official eight-passenger Lincoln limousine, to scan and sign a sheaf of documents or to edit a speech while discoursing on entirely unrelated matters. He also spends a great deal of time on the phone. He has a console of phone buttons, usually lit up like a jukebox, by his desks in City Hall and at the Mansion, as well as an elaborate car-phone setup in the limousine. While about his urban rounds on foot, he is often drawn into a pay-phone booth. (He seems to have a rare instinct for New York pay phones that actually work.)

        .   .   .

Lindsay was born to moderate wealth, the child of a Manhattan banker, and his social credentials are impeccable—private schools, Yale crew, corporate law, even a Virginia wife. Yet Lindsay has established better rapport with the most neglected segment of New York society, the Negroes of Harlem and Bedford-Stuyvesant, than any mayor in history. It is safe to say that in the metropolitan area, he has been the blacks' favorite white after Robert Kennedy. A brave man, he has swiftly plunged into potential riot zones, cooling explosive black tempers. Many believe that Lindsay has been the single most effective force in keeping New York City free of major race upheavals through a period of wholesale urban eruptions.

In turn, the black community has responded to this unlikely "White Knight" with a combination of awe and appreciative respect. "I peeked on him!" cried a Harlem pedestrian as Lindsay's car stopped for a light en route to the Baptist ministers' meeting. Lindsay's performance at the latter was instructive. His speech to the clergymen, chiefly about the effects of the budget squeeze on the ghetto, had a few too many generalities for some of the more militant among them. They rose to demand some hard answers to specific concerns—for example, the fate of vital Harlem Hospital, which underfunded doctors had threatened to close. Lindsay appeared to grow testy. ("I did answer the question but you don't like the answer, so you disagree with it.") The presiding clergyman diplomatically intervened, hailing Lindsay as "courageous." "A lot of his woes," he reminded his audience, "are due to his leaning to interests of our own." From the embarrassed majority came cries of "Amen. . . . That's right. . . . Best mayor we've ever had." . . .

Ironically, as the Lindsay charm has solidified Negro support, it has turned off other ethnic groups, a fact of which he is astutely aware. To the visiting Israeli general, he explained: "I got in trouble with the Jews over the school-strike issue. I may still be." Lindsay had strongly backed community control of schools, which translates into Black Power in New York. Most of the city's unionized schoolteachers are Jewish and suspicious of community control, though Lindsay has always counted on wide Jewish political backing. He is also glumly aware that the chief, obsessive concern of most white ethnic groups, which, despite the political friction, are still a real political factor in New York, is law and order, which they translate into black crime. Most identifiable "ethnic" neighborhoods are now both geographically and ideologically remote from Lindsay's Manhattan, and he approaches them with something of the trepidation of an explorer beating into headhunter territory. Driving to the largely Italian-American small homeowners' meeting in Queens, he wryly suggested to his plainclothes Negro bodyguard: "Ernie, you better duck down. They might think we're trying to integrate the neighborhood." As he entered the meeting hall—a fairly narrow room— the thought crossed his mind (he said later) that it was a good place to get shot. Yet, as he usually does with small groups, Lindsay handled the presumably hostile crowd winningly. After his informal campaign pitch had ended to unexpected applause, he remarked to his aides, "Say, that was a good sign, wasn't it?" as if they were the last people in the world he ever expected to identify with John Lindsay.

. . .

Steady observation indicates that he is an exceptionally intelligent and well-informed officeholder. If he has not proved a complete natural at adapting to the broad politicking aspects of the mayoralty, Lindsay shows a positive zest for the less glamorous administrative side. Despite a series of well-publicized resignations of top administrators whom he had attracted, his gung-ho style has managed to hold many loyal, young, middle-level "urbanists." The Mayor is a fascinated believer in what he calls "the new science of systems approach" to government. He points with particular pride to the people and computers of the Rand Corporation and other "think tanks" that he has contracted to work on the city's problems. "The idea is to surround the whole damn municipality with systems people," he says spiritedly. "We have to harness money and institutional life so that they work together."

Carl Stokes, black mayor of a major American city, has become a symbol of an American Negro who "made it." Born to poor parents, a school drop-out for a time, Stokes rose to be an assistant city prosecutor, a member of the state legislature, and finally mayor of the city in which he was born. As the mayor of a major city, he has all the problems common to mayors of other large cities, including a city that is racially tense.

9

Cleveland's Carl Stokes: Making It

by NEWSWEEK MAGAZINE

"STOKES! Stokes! Stokes!" yelled the crowd. And he appeared, athletically trim, dapper as a duke, Hollywood-handsome, waving and gleaming with victory. "This wonderful moment," he started, and the crowd drowned him out: "Amen, amen!" The voters of Cleveland had just elected Carl Burton Stokes

From "Cleveland's Carl Stokes: Making It," *Newsweek* Magazine, May 26, 1969, pp. 67, 68 and 73. Copyright © 1969 by Newsweek, Inc. Reprinted by permission.

134

the first Negro mayor of a major American city—
and when he could make himself heard, he said:
"This vindicates my faith in the people . . . This is
an American dream."

In the nineteen months since that triumphant peak,
Carl Stokes has had more ups and downs than the
hero of a Victorian novel. . . . Worst of all, Cleveland trembled on the lip of chaos after the assassination of Martin Luther King; for five anguished
nights, Stokes could only prowl the ghetto streets
pleading: "Cool it. Cool it."

That was the first turning point. Miraculously, the
black fury ebbed without a riot like the one that had
swept the Hough ghetto in 1966—and then Stokes
seized the initiative, pulling the city together in its
first real display of civic spirit in decades. He announced the beginning of "Cleveland: Now!", an
ambitious ten- to twelve-year program of civic bet-
terment, and demanded the whole city's support.
The response was overwhelming. "You had to see
the church groups coming in with fruit jars of
pennies, nickels and dimes," Stokes says. "I never
saw community spirit like that before." For three
months, Carl Stokes was a hero in Cleveland—
lauded by the press, idolized in the ghettos, hailed
with astonished joy by the business community. . . .

But the love-in for Carl Stokes is hardly unanimous.
For one thing, his program is still more style than
substance—and Cleveland is still Cleveland, a deeply troubled city with problems that will not be
solved merely with a lift of spirit. More important,
the city is still dominated politically by the hyphen-
ated-American progeny of European immigrants. In
Cleveland, this is called the "cosmo" (short for cos-
mopolitan) or "ethnic" population. At best, it shows
little sympathy for the problems and aspirations of

Negroes; at worst, it provides a hard-core bigot vote that the city's politicians calculate at 20 to 25 per cent of the electorate. And if all this weren't trouble enough for Carl Stokes, he is in some ways his own worst enemy—a fiercely ambitious, highly complex black man whose charismatic charm and real dedication alternate with a cold imperiousness that has alienated some of his friends and splintered his political organization. For all his real achievements, he is waging a tough fight for re-election.

When Stokes took office in 1967, Cleveland had nowhere to go but up. A drab industrial town with a tradition of hard work and little play, the city had been languishing for a quarter of a century under a succession of caretaker mayors. Only four multi-story buildings had been completed in 38 years. Affluent whites and businesses alike were fleeing to the suburbs, and the tax base was shrinking. In fact, just about the only expansion in town was in the black community, which mushroomed from 16 per cent of the population in 1950 to 38 per cent in 1967.

The winding Cuyahoga River, a stream so polluted by industrial wastes that it has been called the only body of water in the world that is a fire hazard, divides the decaying East Side with its predominantly black population from the blue-collar West Side with its 63 ethnic groups. In the black Hough slum, median family income dropped from $4,732 to $3,966 between 1960 and 1965, and families headed by women soared from 23 per cent to 32 per cent.

.   .   .

In a sort of loaves-and-fishes parable, Stokes reports that his Cleveland: Now! program had set aside $500,000 in a fund to aid and start small businesses. But of the first sixteen loans, less than $12,000 came from the fund. "The rest," Stokes says, "came from conventional sources, which had not committed themselves before."

Cleveland: Now! claims many such triumphs. Companies, foundations and individuals have kicked in a total of $4.3 million, to be used as seed money in a ten-year program that will ultimately involve $1.5 billion in Federal, city and private funds. Businessmen have created some 4,500 new jobs. About three dozen summer projects for young people are planned for this year. The program's money has helped to open four day-care centers, supported a summer arts festival, sent children to camp and financed city planning for Federal programs.

. . .

Stokes gives his program the credit for some 2,550 units of housing that will be finished by the end of this year, even though most of them were planned long before Cleveland: Now! was conceived. But the ruse is legitimate, for it is the attitude represented by Stokes and his program that has helped Cleveland to start picking itself up by its tattered shoelaces. Billed as part of the program, a doubling of the city income tax—to a flat rate of 1 per cent—was passed by the City Council last year. Similarly inspired, the city's voters approved increased spending for schools, welfare, street improvements and the city zoo, and passed a $100 million bond issue to cure water pollution. Stokes has also used the program to lure bright new talent to City Hall.

Equally important, says one civic booster, "the new confidence in our city is being translated into bricks and mortar." After the long building drought, there is a small boom in downtown Cleveland: three big office buildings, a luxury apartment building, three convention hotels, three motels and a new

regional post office all are planned or under construction.

All this, of course, is to the good. But will the
style of Stokes and Cleveland: Now! translate into
real achievements? With a touch of skepticism, City
Council president James Stanton says: "If his performance is as good as his public relations, this is
going to be a great city." Some skepticism is certainly justified. Important projects—notably an ambitious new Community Housing Corp.—have lagged
for lack of organization and administrative talent.
In fact, some of Stokes's staunchest supporters fret
that he is not paying enough attention to the details
of running the city. "Carl's long suit is charisma,"
says a longtime friend. "He doesn't like detail."

.   .   .

Soon after his election, the mayor's talent for
cold-eyed calculation began costing him friends and
earning him a reputation for a cardinal political sin:
lack of loyalty. Geraldine Williams, a canny black
politician and close campaign aide, blossomed in
headlines because of her somewhat hazy connection
with a club accused of violating the liquor laws—
and Stokes promptly fired her without even talking
to her. B. Kenneth McGee, a white businessman
who says he lost $10,000 while working in the
Stokes campaign, was rewarded by the cancellation
of a city contract.

At least five other close friends and key aides have
broken with Stokes, including his campaign manager,
Dr. Kenneth Clement. "The mayor," Clement now
says, "has an insufferably low tolerance for private
criticism, which could and should be helpful." . . .

What makes the mayor run? "Carl is poor, and
primarily is concerned with saving himself," hazards
a sympathetic black militant. "It's like shooting

pool—you're in there for yourself. For people who have never been poor, it's difficult to know what that does to you. It kind of explains his fascination with the business community."

Even though his $25,000 salary as mayor is ludicrously low, Carl Stokes is no longer exactly poor. He lives in a large, comfortable house on the last street in Cleveland before the city limits. His attractive wife, Shirley, stays out of the limelight; 10-year-old Carl Jr. attends private school (daughter Cordi, 8, is in the public system). The mayor collects antiques and delights in his modish suits, monogrammed shirts and expensive cigars. To Stokes, the new life style is a matter of course. "We had a chance," he says simply.

Clearly, it is a life style that his black constituents don't begrudge. "Every black person in town feels he has a piece of him," says Negro councilman George Forbes. "Carl Stokes is what they want their child to be." Children, black and white, also love the mayor—and mob him joyfully wherever he goes.

·   ·   ·

In this selection the author describes
how the Mayor of Boston has tried to
make his city government more responsive to the needs of the people and more
aware of their gripes and grievances.

10

Little City Halls

by ALAN LUPO

. . . .

EAST BOSTON two years ago preferred Louise Day
Hicks, darling of the white ethnics, to Kevin H.
White by more than 300 votes. In that racially tinted
campaign, White squeezed by with a 12,429-vote
margin and in the process learned a few things about
urban America.

From "Little City Halls," by Alan Lupo, *City* Magazine,
April 1969, pp. 5–8. Copyright © 1969 by the National Urban
Coalition. Reprinted by permission of *City* Magazine.

. . .

White has said that the "greatest domestic crisis in America today is the failure of cities to respond to the human needs of its citizens, and this is precisely the problem we are attacking." His "little city halls" program is new and shaky, but it has demonstrated the potential for dealing effectively with interdepartmental cooperation, community participation, liaison among city, state, and federal government agencies, and civil service reform. Also, if it works to any appreciable degree, it could become an important political asset to a mayor.

The mayoral campaign of 1967, coinciding with a local newspaper series on Boston's neighborhoods, made it very clear that Boston's next mayor would have to find new ways of dealing with the city's 517,000 whites and its 100,000 blacks, Puerto Ricans, and Chinese. . . .

After White's election, a brain trust of sorts, including a black antipoverty worker from the South End (a community of 42—count 'em, 42—ethnic groups), a local Irish political adviser, ex-Kennedy aide Adam Yarmolinsky, former California finance director Hale Champion and others, began discussing what kind of device to suggest to the mayor. . . .

A mayor, insisted Champion, needs a monitoring system. "He needs to have these problems raised for his attention at an early stage before they come to an impasse. He needs to assure the citizens they have legitimate complaints.

"You can't fight City Hall, not through individual city departments. You have to fight it through elected officials. You have to come to the city council or the mayor to get attention—a system which doesn't solve the problems between citizens and bureaucra-

Negro and white children protest the cut in O.E.O. funds in Roxbury, Massachusetts, that closed down their tutoring program. (Eric Brown, Monkmeyer)

DON'T YOU WANT MY CHILD [EARN]

[The More money you GIVE] The more we LEARN

cy, for decision by elected officials doesn't work very well."

. . .

Today, the city runs ten centers in trailers and old municipal buildings and plans to establish three more. By early February, they had processed more than 4,900 written requests and complaints and had handled thousands of visitors and phone calls.

In many cases, it was simply a matter of referring a citizen to the correct agency or handing someone a veteran's bonus form or civil service application. These are the bread-and-butter services of government, the kind of requests that often involve the average citizen in dozens of phone calls and frustrating referrals.

. . .

Most problems, however, reflect the ceaseless struggle between Man, the urban animal, and the multitude of city, state, and federal zookeepers who exist, theoretically, to serve him. With the decline of the wardheelers and the growth of bureaucracy— a bureaucracy burdened in Massachusetts with an antiquated civil service system—the urban dweller often is seething with anger at a government he does not understand.

This is why the White administration has the federal government send social security workers to the little city halls. This is why it is experimenting with a multi-service approach in the South End center, which has, in addition to the regular staff,

143

Our cities must be made pleasant, not just livable. (UPI)

Communities are becoming more organized in an effort to assert their constitutional rights. (Rogers, Monkmeyer)

a full-time social security representative, a health clinic, a library, recreation facilities, and 14 housing inspectors. This is why most of the East Boston staff speak Italian, why four of the South End staff speak Spanish, why one Mattapan worker speaks Yiddish.

No responsible city official is suggesting that any of this will prevent trouble, a spilling over of that anger and frustration into the streets.

.   .   .

But the little city halls at least serve as an early warning system to allow the mayor and his staff a few days or a few hours to prepare some kind of response. This is a luxury in today's city government.

These days in once-apathetic East Boston, strange things have been happening. Women and children have physically blocked dump trucks from using a street as a route to the airport. A civic association, led by priests, has submitted its own package of state legislation to curb the powers of the port authority, which operates the airport. Residents have joined a racially integrated alliance of neighborhoods calling for a halt in highway and tunnel planning and new mass transit priorities.

Very much in the middle of all this activity is the little city hall staff, not manipulating, but there, staying on top of the situation, ready to decode the signals of alienation for the mayor, ready to break down for him and the neighborhood the social, political, and economic alternatives posed by each crisis.

If the urban experts need a name for that process, they might call it democracy.

In this selection the writer describes what
determined citizens can do with public
spirit but without public funds to develop play areas they sorely need.

11

50 Miniparks
in Three Weeks

by THE AMERICAN CITY MAGAZINE

.   .   .

WHAT BEGAN in Memphis on a rat-burrowed, de-
bris-laden, weed-choked lot to the rhythmic encour-
agement of a soul band the rainy morning of May
11, 1968, is best explained as the chemistry of
imagination, cooperation, dedication and hard work

148

The government is too often bogged down in red tape.
Improvements must be made immediately. Citizens' committees are seeking more autonomy in community affairs.
They are fortunate when the government is enlightened
enough to support them. (George Favre)

interacting to produce a community benefit—playgrounds in parkless neighborhoods.

At about 10 A.M. that Saturday, approximately 150 adults and youngsters of all ages began wielding hoes, rakes and shovels; piling wheelbarrows high with trash; manipulating weed-cutters, while sanitation crews hauled away old tires, raw garbage, broken glass and boards, abandoned shopping carts, auto springs and other collected debris, and volunteers operated earthmoving equipment.

With the lot cleared and graded, the youngsters moved on to clean other areas of the neighborhood. The remaining adults set up volley ball and badminton courts, basketball backboards, swings; anchored tetherball standards and installed hockey boxes, to create the first of Memphis' "Cleani-Mini" parks. Elapsed time for the entire operation: 4½ hours.

The next Saturday, following a similar procedure, five more miniparks came into being at different locations in the city. Within three weeks, Memphians created 50 "instant" playgrounds—without the assistance of city, county, state or federal funds.

Motivation for the minipark boom stemmed from the Clean-Up, Paint-Up, Fix-Up, Plant-Up Committee of the Memphis City Beautiful Commission, which took the first step by facing realities: (1) the toll from a devastating sanitation strike had left Memphis filthy; (2) neighborhood and community spirit were non-existent, and (3) fear, tension, distrust and animosity reigned as a result of the assassination of Dr. Martin Luther King, Jr. . . .

An extraordinary activity, the kind that would galvanize the citizens of Memphis into a cohesive, constructive force working for a common goal, was requisite.

·   ·   ·

The committee established guidelines for the playgrounds. However, it left the real responsibility of creating and maintaining the miniparks in the hands of the residents of the local neighborhoods in which parks were to be and are now located.

. .   .   .

To meet necessary legal requirements and possible eventualities, the committee created Cleani-Mini Park, Inc., chartered as a non-profit organization, to lease lots from property owners for $1 per year (contracts include a 30-day cancellation clause and an option to renew) and to offer a degree of protection for property owners, in the form of a blanket insurance policy (purchased by the corporation) for bodily injury and property damage liability. In addition, each miniplayground has been placed under the insurance coverage of the City Park Commission.

As news of the project spread, private citizens and local businesses donated funds (individual contributions ranged from $1 to $5,000) and services.

A local construction company loaned earthmoving and materials handling equipment to rid lots of layers of debris and to grade them, when necessary. An exterminating company, as a contributed service, went into each lot prior to cleaning to comb it for underground rat burrows. It continues to provide free rat extermination and control.

A Memphis advertising agency exercised its communications expertise as a public service. By doing so, it insured coverage by newspapers, radio and TV stations, nationally as well as locally.

. .   .   .

Some trucks were volunteered for trash pickup, but the city's sanitation department picked up and hauled most of the trash during the Saturday of each park-area cleanup. The committee paid the hourly wages of the crews.

Park department personnel guided the selection and the purchase of play equipment, which had to be both durable and safe. Crews set all equipment in concrete. Sears, which made volleyball and basketball sets available at a generous discount, installed them free in the first six parks. Miracle Equipment Company donated a fiberglass slide, round picnic table and park bench. The swing sets purchased from Miracle for the minipark program were 8-foot-high swings with four seats per set of swings.

.   .   .

Children in the neighborhoods did all the painting. Sometimes the activity took on the look of a psychedelic paint-in; always it proved a fun experience. Members of the local Paint and Varnish Association donated the paint.

Momentum continues. Memphis now has 58 miniparks—eight more neighborhoods organized, raised the money for and built miniparks by themselves. Park sizes vary from a strip of land 40x120 feet to more than an acre. The average cost of converting a vacant lot into a minipark approaches $350 to $400.

.   .   .

William E. Shelton, III, chairman of the Memphis Clean-Up, Fix-Up, Paint-Up, Plant-Up Committee and senior vice-president of Leader Federal Savings and Loan Association of Memphis, says that the miniparks represent an involvement of approximately 7,000 people. He conservatively estimates that the combined value of volunteered land, services, work, and monetary donations totals $1½ million. "And," he says, "not only have vast areas of low-income neighborhoods been cleared up and small parks established where needed most, but the Cleani-Mini parks have served as catalysts in developing cooperation among citizens, a greater pride in neighborhood and a sense of community. The residual effects include the flowers planted, the fences painted, and the houses repaired."

Every day thousands of workers from the suburbs travel into the central city to work in offices and factories. Should these people contribute to the cost of running the central city? This selection tells why some of America's larger cities are asking commuters for fiscal help—in fact, why they are demanding it.

12

Commuters and City Income Taxes

by JAC FRIEDGUT

COMMUTERS' importance to the economic base of cities is well known. According to one study, they account for close to two fifths of personal income in Cincinnati. In New York and Philadelphia, about a quarter of wages and salaries goes to them.

From "Commuters and City Income Taxes," by Jac Friedgut, *Nation's Business*, October 1969, p. 66. Copyright © *Nation's Business*—the Chamber of Commerce of the United States. Reprinted by permission.

(Sam Falk, Monkmeyer)

More than 170 cities and numerous smaller towns levy personal income taxes. They are predominantly in the quadrant of the U. S. that includes New York, Philadelphia, Pittsburgh, Detroit, Louisville and Cleveland. To the west and south, income taxes are not imposed by cities, with a few exceptions such as St. Louis and Kansas City, Mo., and Gadsden, Ala.

Nearly all cities with income taxes levy them on nonresidents, though in some, nonresidents are taxed at a different rate. While New York City residents pay on a graduated scale running from 0.4 per cent to 2 per cent, commuters pay a flat 0.25 per cent. In Detroit and other Michigan cities, the resident rate of 1 per cent is halved for nonresidents. And when a commuter's income is taxed by the community where he lives, he may be entitled to a credit against taxes in the community where he works.

The nonresident argues that a commuter levy is taxation without representation. Meanwhile, his own suburban real estate taxes rise. In addition, he is subjected to ever-increasing state taxes, part of which are used by the states to help meet city problems such as welfare.

Besides, the commuter's employer is being taxed by the city. If nonresidents staged a mass boycott and quit their jobs in the city, the affected firms might move, contract in size, or even go out of business, with corresponding reductions in the city's tax take. Actually, it is unlikely commuters would cut off their noses to spite their faces, but the resentment is there.

Businesses are concerned. When New York's Mayor John Lindsay proposed a graduated city income tax on residents and commuters alike, the New

York Chamber of Commerce argued: "It does not appear reasonable to subject these non-New York residents to the heavy burden which would result from a progressive-rate local income tax."

However, both the Chamber and the New York Commerce and Industry Association would have gone along with a payroll tax (about 1 per cent). As it turned out, the commuters, with a flat 0.25 per cent rate, did better than expected.

The arguments advanced by the cities generally revolve around those benefits they allegedly provide for the commuters and for the surrounding region as a whole.

As an example, the $6.1 billion expense budget for New York City for the 1969 fiscal year was allocated something like this:

Program	Per cent
Human resources	25.5
Education	24.3
Health services	11.2
Debt service	11.1
Administration of justice	9.3
Fire protection	3.7
Environmental protection	3.6
Transportation	3.2
Recreation and culture	1.9
All other	6.2
Total	100.0

Of these items, the commuter clearly benefits directly from programs accounting for 21.7 per cent of the total: administration of justice (police), fire protection, environmental protection (air pollution control, etc.), transportation, and recreation and culture.

As for health services, the amount of benefit is not clear. Commuters generally cannot qualify for free services at city hospitals. On the other hand, if city health officials prevent a major epidemic, they provide an invaluable service to nonresidents.

Debt service, likewise, is a mixed bag. Paying off capital improvements on traffic control should be of direct interest to the commuter. However, he might feel less responsibility for servicing debt on school construction.

In the "all other" category, the commuter could be said to benefit from some expenditures, such as those for economic development (0.1 per cent). However, he is not the immediate beneficiary of others, such as housing (0.4 per cent).

The commuter is not involved directly in two major categories which account for virtually half of the city's budget: the human resources (welfare and welfare-related) and education programs. However, at least in theory, these programs are of some indirect benefit to him in that they aim at upgrading the quality of life which constitutes his working-time milieu.

One fact is clear. As urban burdens grow, with the disadvantaged concentrated more and more in the inner areas, cities will need substantial fiscal help. The magnitude of the problem—and the help required—goes far beyond the question of taxing commuters. It is a problem of national scope, and will require basic restructuring of federal-state-local fiscal relationships.

Megalopolis is the name given to the super-city from Boston, Massachusetts, to Washington, D.C. This, the author describes as the "Main Street" of the nation, the heart of its financial, business, industrial, and cultural complex. Since Megalopolis crosses state lines and embraces thousands of different forms of local government, a host of problems are created.

13

The Challenge of Megalopolis

by WOLF VON ECKARDT

LOCAL government has become big business. Both budgets and the number of employees have rapidly grown in the twentieth century and so has the indebtedness.

From *The Challenge of Megalopolis*, by Wolf von Eckardt (New York: The Macmillan Company, 1964), pp. 114–17. Copyright © 1964 by The Macmillan Company. Based on the original study of Jean Gootman. Reprinted by permission of The Macmillan Company.

America is being buried in concrete. Many people feel more government money should go toward preserving our natural resources and insuring green, open spaces for the future, rather than building more highways. (Hays, Monkmeyer)

The expenditures of local government in recent years have far surpassed those of state governments.

Yet local revenues are inadequate to cover local expenditures. The local governments have therefore turned to the state's treasury for a share of the funds collected from state taxes.

The states, in turn, receive financial help from federal funds.

In this fiscal doubleplay, state and federal contributions combined to make up 26 per cent of all local revenues.

The local authorities are, however, somewhat limited in their freedom to spend this good quarter of their income. Congressional and state legislation earmarks it for specific purposes such as highway construction, public schools, hospitals, health and other services.

Another limitation on a locality's freedom to dispose of its budget is the fact that much outside help is given to supplement specific programs. Thus localities often launch such programs to get the assistance even though some other venture might be more important.

The extent of outside aid granted local governments varies considerably and bears no relation to actual need. The reason is that in most state legislatures, notably those of New York, Pennsylvania and Maryland, the rural areas have long held the balance of power. Rural communities are therefore receiving far more aid than their share of the state's population warrants.

Nationally speaking, school districts fare best. On the average they receive 43 per cent of their revenue from outside sources. Counties follow closely, with 38 per cent. Townships depend on grants and shared taxes for 25 per cent of their

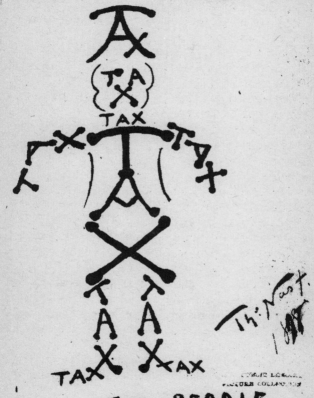

THE PEOPLE.

(Thomas Nast, The New York Public Library, Picture Collection)

Baltimore inner-city children enjoy a few features of a "Fun Wagon" sponsored by the Baltimore Bureau of Recreation. (Monkmeyer)

funds. But cities obtain only about 14 per cent on the average. The larger the city the smaller the percentage of outside help it receives.

Although these are national ratios, the implications for Megalopolis are clear. Neither the large central cities nor the metropolitan areas are receiving a fair share of the financial help they desperately need.

The central cities need it because they are losing resident population but must still provide services for commuting and visiting outsiders. And the metropolitan suburbs need it because their great influx of new residents requires more and more costly services spread out over an increasingly sprawling area. They try to expand their tax base by attracting more people and industry. But to serve these, they must, of course, first invest money in new schools, roads, and sewers. The return on this investment in the form of additional tax comes in much later.

Despite federal aid, state and local taxes are therefore constantly going up. Inequities and difficulties arise. One is that some Megalopolitan states have an income tax which they levy not only on their own residents but also on income earned by people who live in another state. Another is the distribution of state-collected tax money to the cities.

New York State, for instance, assigns New York City a share of its revenue, according to the city's proportion of the Census population. Since that population has been declining, the aid the city receives is also shrinking. However, expenditures for urban renewal, education, and welfare must, of course, be increased if the city wants to arrest even further population losses.

Cities are centers. That means they must serve a wide area around them and not just their own residents. Their well-being affects the entire surrounding area, transcending state lines, just as the heart affects the health of the entire body.

Cities are furthermore expected to provide not only the necessities but such institutions as parks, zoological and botanical gardens, museums and libraries, which do not bring any revenue but cost a great deal.

This is particularly true of Washington, D.C., which, as the national capital, must serve the entire nation. The whole nation must therefore share in the cost of its efficient operation.

The revenues American cities can raise on their own are entirely insufficient to meet these responsibilities. They rely almost exclusively on the property tax. The proportion of income from this source has recently been declining. New sources have had to be developed, but such new taxes and fees have so far failed to solve the problem.

Proposals to increase this tax, as land values increase, would bring little relief. For the large cities, which have the greatest need for increased income, also have the highest proportion of tax-exempt property.

In New York City, for instance, more than 30 per cent of all real property belongs to the city itself or to other tax-exempt institutions. This includes parks, schools, public buildings, public works, public housing, sewerage systems, hospitals, harbor piers and airports. Other properties are tax-exempt because they belong to the state or federal governments or to religious, educational, philanthropic and other non-profit institutions. In Boston this percentage is even higher—36.2 per cent. In Providence it is 24 per cent, in Philadelphia 22 per cent, and in Baltimore 18 per cent.

There is no question that the limits of local taxation have been reached. The urbanization and economic integration of Megalopolis make more state and federal aid to its large centers imperative.

Metro is a form of government that attempts to embrace an entire metropolitan region. Here the author explains how we are moving in that direction.

14 | # More Metropolitan Government Than You Think

by WILLIAM S. FOSTER

THE great philosopher-comedian-cowboy Will Rogers used to tell us that "All he knew was what he read in the newspapers." If all he knew about a metropolitan approach to urban services and facilities was what he read in the so-called popular

From "More Metropolitan Government Than You Think," by William S. Foster, *The American City* Magazine, August 1963, p. 9. Copyright © 1963 by Buttenheim Publishing Corporation. Reprinted by permission of Buttenheim Publishing Corporation.

press, the odds are that he would be wrong. If all he knew was what some of the self-appointed "experts" on urban affairs tell him in certain books and articles, he would be even more wrong.

The Metro proposal is not some new panacea like the Salk vaccine that automatically will cure our urban ills. We have had many examples of metropolitan government in one form or another for years.

The most perfect is in our 50th state, in the land of pineapples and hula dances. Honolulu's governmental structure embraces the entire island of Oahu. This includes two great mountain ranges, rice paddies, plantations, great military bases, and probably a half dozen communities that would be identified as independent municipalities elsewhere. The Honolulu that most think of occupies only a small portion of the southern fringe of the island.

Moreover the state never has had any governmental unit smaller than the county in its history as part of the United States. Nor is there any particularly strong movement in Hawaii to form municipalities as the rest of the nation knows them.

New York City is another pertinent example. As long ago as the turn of the century, civic leaders drew together a group of independent cities to form what we now know as New York, never dreaming that the city ever would outgrow those boundaries. The fact that New York did outgrow is a lesson in itself.

As most know, New York City formed itself into five boroughs, each with considerable independence. However, this did not automatically bring coordination and general overall management. For example, over 60 years had to pass before the engineers in each borough would design sewers with the same design tables and formulas.

San Francisco for many years has been a city and county, in the best of Metro concepts, but it also outgrew its borders. And who would not recognize that Los Angeles' far-reaching boundaries are a vigorous effort to provide metropolitan organization to this fast-growing area. Now Oklahoma City has adopted the same practical policy, as has Houston. Miami's Dade County Metro blazed no really new trails.

And to provide specific services, cities have been thinking in terms of the metropolitan concept for years. The Chicago Sanitary District, organized in 1899, reaches far beyond Chicago to serve virtually all of Cook County.

The Washington Suburban Sanitary Commission, serving an area of 427 square miles adjacent to the District of Columbia, created 45 years ago, provides water, sewerage and refuse collection and disposal services. The Metropolitan District of Hartford (Conn.) came into being in 1929 to provide water and sewerage services to Hartford and six suburban towns. The younger Allegheny County Sanitation Authority provides sewerage services to the Pittsburgh metropolitan area. The East Bay Municipal Utilities District for many years has served a number of municipalities in Oakland, California, area. Boston has a metropolitan transit authority. There are many other examples.

Admittedly, a metropolitan approach becomes particularly difficult when the growing urban area finds itself enmeshed in state boundaries. New York, Philadelphia, Chicago, Cincinnati, Memphis, St. Louis, Kansas City, Washington, D.C., all have this sort of obstacle to overcome. Even here, agencies

such as the Port of New York Authority reach
across state boundaries, although not in a way that
entirely satisfies all. And one or two interstate sanitation authorities show that even a state line can
be breached.

Some believe that regional planning is the answer to the chaos in our cities. They believe that uncontrolled and unplanned growth of cities is one of the most important causes of our problems today. The author of this selection says that local representatives must be permitted to plan city and regional land use for the benefit of all the people, and that land in the urban areas must no longer be used by private businessmen for profit motives.

15

Cities Grow A-Go-Go

by GEORGE H. FAVRE

. . . URBAN sprawl is choking every major metropolitan area of the United States. The process follows a recognizable pattern. Small businesses—gas stations, motels, restaurants—seek cheaper land on the metropolitan fringe. Their pop architecture is de-

From "Cities Grow A-Go-Go," by George H. Favre, *The Christian Science Monitor*, November 1–3, 1969. Copyright © 1969 by The Christian Science Publishing Society. All rights reserved. Reprinted by permission of *The Christian Science Monitor*.

Planned communities provide better environments.
(George Favre)

Too much land is mistreated in America. (Wide World)

signed to attract the motorist's eye. At first these developments are widely spaced, but soon the gaps are filled. Architecture and billboards compete for attention with increasing blatancy.

Sprawl, as its name implies, is planless. It occurs as a result of decisions by small-business men, and its basis is economics—the cheapest land with the most exposure to traveled highways. Thus metropolitan development is "planned" by entrepreneurs who neither know nor care what or how they plan.

Housing developers are not far behind. They build far away from these first installations because home buyers don't want gas stations and taverns in their neighborhood. Patches of land are left undeveloped, held off the market by owners who hope to make a windfall profit.

As the process goes on, subdivisions become increasingly remote. Public services—roads, water, sewers, drains, sidewalks, schools, police and fire protection—are poor. As development solidifies, these services must be upgraded at inflated prices. The new homeowners bear the burden.

The contrast between the European and American experience in urban development hinges on how people view land and its development. In the long history of Europe, land has been held in its entirety by kings and emperors or in huge estates by the church or the nobility.

In the earlier centuries, these landowners planned entire cities—London, Paris, Rome, and dozens of others. Today, European city and national governments do the planning. But they do plan, comprehensively and positively.

In the United States, land is regarded as a commodity, to be bought and sold for maximum profit. Land development is a speculative venture. In this

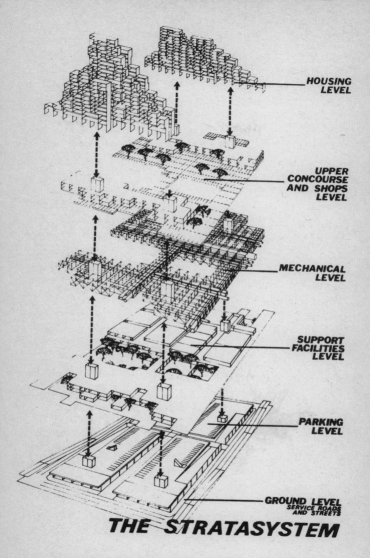

HOUSING LEVEL

UPPER CONCOURSE AND SHOPS LEVEL

MECHANICAL LEVEL

SUPPORT FACILITIES LEVEL

PARKING LEVEL

GROUND LEVEL
SERVICE ROADS AND STREETS

THE STRATASYSTEM

Some architects are developing fantastic planned communities for the future. (The Eggers Partnership)

capitalist society, rapidly devolving toward a welfare state, land ownership and development is one of the last bastions of laissez-faire.

Planning in the United States is defensive and negative. Zoning laws and building codes are "thou shalt not" proscriptions. Most planning is confined to the major cities, which are already built up, which means planning is after-the-fact. There is little regional planning, and nothing that could remotely be called a national plan—despite the fact that Congress passes laws and establishes new agencies that, in an uncoordinated way, affect millions of planning decisions quite as much as an organized plan would.

In Europe, the master plan is a document put together by sociologists, political scientists, educators, ecologists, and transportation experts as well as physical planners. Many of these master plans cover far greater areas than a single city. Paris has a regional plan. So do Stockholm and the Randstad (ring cities) of Holland.

Planning in the United States is still a relatively new idea and suspect. Even a sophisticated city like New York is only now, in 1969, getting ready to adopt a master plan.

Even where master plans exist in American cities, they are often put on the shelf for years and ignored. In most European cities, they are continually revised, from year to year or even month to month.

There is even a move afoot in the United States to do away with master plans as unrealistic. The arguments are that these plans are ignored or that urban growth patterns are too complex to plan.

Can reversion to laissez-faire solve America's problems? Nothing about the condition of American cities today suggests this is the case.

Europe's experience, on the other hand, suggests

strongly that farsighted planning, incorporating the best insights of many disciplines and balancing private interests, can do much to keep the growth of cities orderly, efficient, beautiful, and humane. . . .

Notes

Suggested Reading List

Index

Notes

THE PROBLEM AND THE CHALLENGE

1. Robert C. Wood, *1,400 Governments* (New York: Doubleday Anchor Books, 1964), p. 1 (originally Harvard University Press, 1961).
2. Based on Wallace S. Sayer and Herbert Kaufman, *Governing New York City* (New York: Russell Sage Foundation, 1960), pp. 60–63.
3. *Ibid.,* p. 62.
4. Seymour Freedgood, "New Strength in City Hall," in *The Exploding Metropolis,* by the Editors of *Fortune* (New York: Doubleday Anchor Books, 1958), p. 85.
5. Gordon Mitchell, *Sick Cities* (New York: The Macmillan Company, 1963), p. 257.
6. Quoted in *ibid.,* p. 300.
7. *Ibid.,* p. 256.
8. Melvin M. Webber, "The Post-City Age," *Daedalus,* Fall 1968, Vol. 97, No. 4, p. 1093.
9. *Ibid.*

Suggested Reading List

1. Bailey, Helen Miller. *Your American Government*. London: Longmans, 1956.

2. Beard, Charles A. *American Government and Politics*. New York: The Macmillan Company, 1949.

3. Commager, Henry Steele. *The Great Constitution*. Indianapolis: Bobbs-Merrill, 1961.

4. DiMond, Stanley E., and Elmer F. Pflieger. *Civics for Citizens*. Philadelphia: J. B. Lippincott, 1965.

5. Herber, Lewis. *Crisis in Our Cities*. Englewood Cliffs, N.J.: Prentice-Hall, Inc., 1967.

6. Kent, Frank E. *The Great Game of Politics*. Buffalo, N.Y.: Smith, Keynes and Marshall, 1959.

7. Leinwand, Gerald. *The American Constitution: A Tutor-Text*. New York: Doubleday, 1964.

8. Levine, Naomi. *Schools in Crisis*. New York: Popular Library, 1969.

9. McDonald, Austin F. *American City Government and Administration*. New York: Crowell, 1956.

10. Martin, Roscoe C. *The Cities and the Federal System*. New York: Atherton Press, 1965.

Index

GENERAL EDITOR

Gerald Leinwand is Professor of Education and Chairman of the Department of Education at the Bernard M. Baruch College of the City University of New York. Dr. Leinwand received his B.A., M.S., and Ph.D. degrees from New York University and an M.A. from Columbia University. In addition to numerous magazine articles, he is the author of *The Pageant of World History, The American Constitution: A Tutor-Text,* and a college text *Teaching History and the Social Studies in Secondary Schools.*